FOLIO

Department of Architecture
Florida International University
2014 - 2015

This yearbook was published by
The Department of Architecture
College of Architecture + The Arts
Florida International University
2014-2015.

The Department of Architecture
College of Architecture + The Arts
Florida International University

ISBN: 978-1-939621-34-4

Editors
Henry Rueda
Alastair Gordon
Marny Pereda

Graphic Design
Fonte Design
Raul Lira

Production Team
Folio Class
Spring & Summer 2015

Printed in the United States of America on
Heavyweight paper

The Department of Architecture
College of Architecture + The Arts
Florida International University
Modesto A. Maidique Campus
Paul L. Cejas School of Architecture Building
11200 SW 8th Street PCA 280
Miami, Florida 33199
305 348 1323
http://carta.fiu.edu/architecture/

Miami Beach Urban Studios
420 Lincoln Rd. Suite 440
Miami Beach, Florida 33139
305 535 1463
http://mbus.fiu.edu/

Contents

Message from the Chair
Jason R. Chandler, A.I.A

Chair & Associate Professor
Department of Architecture
College of Architecture + The Arts
Florida International University

The work of the Department of Architecture at Florida International University inextricably binds itself to the ever-changing dynamic of Miami. While this sprawling metropolis establishes itself as an international center for architecture and art, it does so sitting precariously on tenuous environmental and economic ground. Many of the world's most noted architects are working in Miami and providing our students with remarkable projects to experience firsthand. Our students are also witnessing a boom-and-bust economy of speculative development and the impact of coastal flooding. This Janus-faced city of inspiration and challenge parallels the paired mission of the department - to ethically train practitioners and inspire new visionaries.

To satisfy this mission, the department offers the Master of Architecture, which is organized into two distinct, yet complementary spheres: the core and elective. In the core curriculum, students gain the requisite skills and training to establish a critical knowledge base for self-directed study. Our diverse faculty offers a range of research and pedagogic tracks: from the development of a building detail to the planning of the infrastructure of a city, for example. The elective track culminates in our master project sequence of a seminar and studio, directed by a single faculty member with a specific research focus. The core and elective curricula reflect the daily work of the architect, the ultimate multi-tasker and a person who simultaneously solves immediate problems while envisioning a better future. School is only a small portion of the life of the architect. In the most ideal world, it is the beginning of a lifelong education.

Within the College of Architecture + The Arts (CARTA), the Department of Architecture is composed of 19 full-time faculty members, 30 adjunct faculty and over 450 students. We work in the award-winning Paul L. Cejas School of Architecture building designed by Bernard Tschumi. This mini-campus houses our studios, classrooms, offices, and three labs: the Fabrication Lab, the Structures and Environmental Technologies (SET) Lab, and the Digital Lab. In addition, our faculty and students work at our college's 16,000-square-foot Miami Beach Urban Studios (MBUS) located on Lincoln Road. Both of these facilities firmly establish our program within the expansive metropolis of Miami.

This first edition of *Folio* represents a snapshot of one academic year. It does not fully capture the intensity of work or the dynamic energy of our students and faculty, yet it provides a look into the department's diversity of design, research, and creative activity. To establish this new vantage, students created this publication in a series of classes led by Henry Rueda, visiting assistant professor, in collaboration with Alastair Gordon, Dean's Distinguished Fellow, 2014-2015. Students reconsidered what a journal for an architecture program could be and expanded this well-worn type by representing our program as an engaged event enriched by the numerous parallel activities of the city in which we live.

The department's mission and the value of making a book is a preoccupation of *Folio*. Its content reflects many student and faculty conversations and prompts real questions about who we are. We have, for two years, posted eFolio on our department's website. This magazine, published once a semester, satisfies the need to post our work in a timely fashion for a vast audience. It is infinity accessible and embraces the energy of new media. So, why do we choose to make Folio? Folio was made to create a physical archive of the ephemeral efforts of our department. In it, you will find student work, faculty research and essays about the life of the department and Miami. Designed as an object that occupies space, we introduce Folio into the world to celebrate the mission of our program and to establish it as the center of architectural discourse in the region.

I thank the faculty and students for their support and energy in making this publication. I extend a special thanks to Henry Rueda for spearheading this project and for his extraordinary effort to make it happen, to Raul Lira for his design of the layout, and to Alastair Gordon for his expertise and provocation to make *Folio* unique and timely. I thank the College of Architecture + The Arts's Dean Brian Schriner for his support of this publication and Ambassador Paul L. Cejas for his continued support of the department and college.

Welcome to the first issue of *Folio*!

Editor's Statement
Henry Rueda

Visiting Assistant Professor
Professor Department of Architecture

Since the beginning of this project: *Folio*, we have been questioning the relevance of an academic annual publication. Collecting, archiving, categorizing and filing had been part of our duties. In this digital era, there are many paths, we stumbled upon this two: How to produce, file and archive new content, new architectural data? How to store a library of concepts, diagrams, drawings, renderings, models at the same time of fast growing social media platforms? Is it relevant to produce a book in a time when a 3 minute's video is too extent to maintain the attention of the spectator. Sometimes we have to call it: "a physical book" since the traditional definition allows for many digital formats and representations.

In times of unedited imagery, a selective discussion of produced work in a well curated printed document, will prevail over the frenetic experience of ephemeral blogs and rapidly fading websites, we are certain of this.

Miami is in constant transformation and its growth needs the voices of new generations of architects. The role of our school is immense; not only attending local issues, but also in welcoming and preparing students from around the globe. FIU has the privilege and responsibility to attend all of the Americas; this makes this publication connect our communities and establish a platform for cross geographical collaborations.

The work that our Faculty and Students produce in the School of Architecture is as broad as the geographical origins of all its members. The projects and essays presented on this book had been selected and classified for discussion and analysis. It is past work, yet it engages the reader on the future of our School. Navigation around our database can be easily done through our various online platforms, Facebook, Twitter and Instagram pages, but the importance of Folio, relies on its ability not only to produce new content, but to discern this production and provoke critical positions from our readers.

The possibility of dissecting the school for the first time, was a benefit that I shared with our MAA student Marny Pereda, who was instrumental in the making of this project and had the stamina to continue on this long race.

Folio is not only a publication of student work, it is also a position on topics around the City and the Miami Matters essays and interviews, aim to engage a broader audience into the dialogue.

It is an exciting time to be at FIU!

Master's Projects
Alfredo Andia
Malik Benjamin
Jaime Canaves
Eric Goldemberg
Marilys Nepomech
Eric Peterson
Camilo Rosales

FIU Department of Architecture
Master's Projects

This work represents the efforts of our diverse and talented
graduating class. This year, we had seven studios. Collectively,
these studios reflect the department's wide range of creative
research topics. In these studios, each faculty member
establishes a pedagogic subject for students to develop
individually or in teams.

These topics represent issues that confront both academia and
the profession and serve as a vision of the complex issues that
our graduates will encounter when they leave the school.

Jason R. Chandler, A.I.A.
Chair, Department of Architecture

Alfredo Andia
Art-In-Residence Vestals

The consumption of art has grown drastically in the past two decades. This boom has been escorted with the explosive expansion of major museums, art fairs, galleries, art collectors, and record breaking prices for art pieces. What about the artist?

In this studio, we speculate that this "Art-Boom" will transform again as art institutions and art patrons will start backing fresh and larger new art-in-residence programs. Art-in-residence programs allow an artist or group of artists to live, work, and exhibit their work in a particular place. We claim that architecture will be a critical factor for the visibility and prestige of these emerging art-in-residence programs. This studio explores how architecture can say something fundamental about how humans live. The main human-space tactic the students consider during their Master Project are based on field explorations they developed in one-to-one installations in the previous semester. These explorations are, by their nature, unequivocally "pure" and absolutely "useless." The explorations of the "useless" have been at the epicenter of architectural progress. "Useless" exercises such as the Barcelona Pavilion, the fish sculptures of Frank Gehry, the sketches of the domino plan, and books such as Delirious New York are a small array of examples of "non-useful" projects that have sparked significant architectural development throughout the recent history of the discipline.

The "Vestals" were the virgin priestesses of Vesta that cultivated the continued fire in ancient Roman religion. These structures are the Vestals of the now.

Ksenia Kosykh

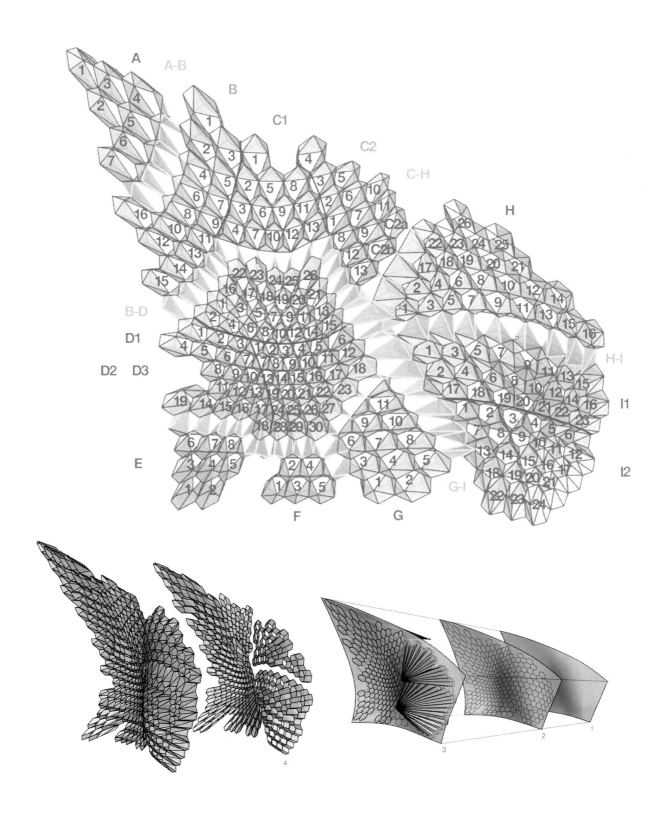

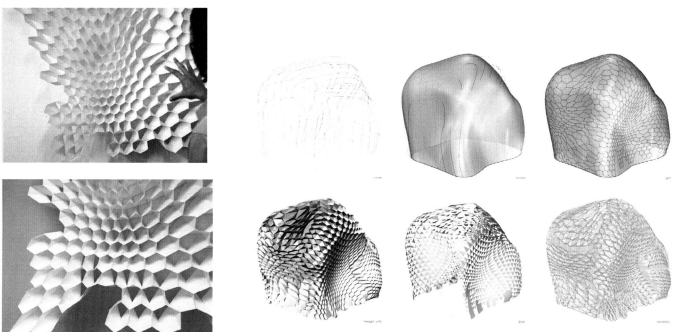

Haley Perry

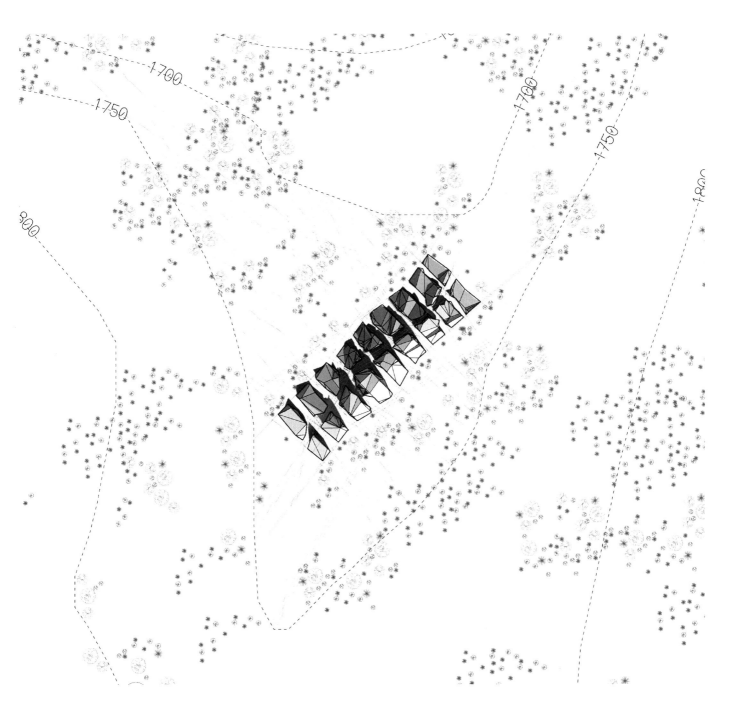

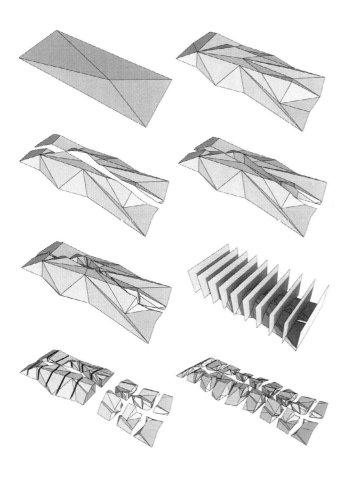

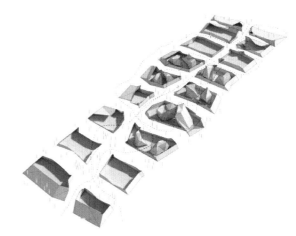

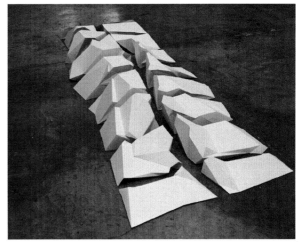

Jacqueline Rowe

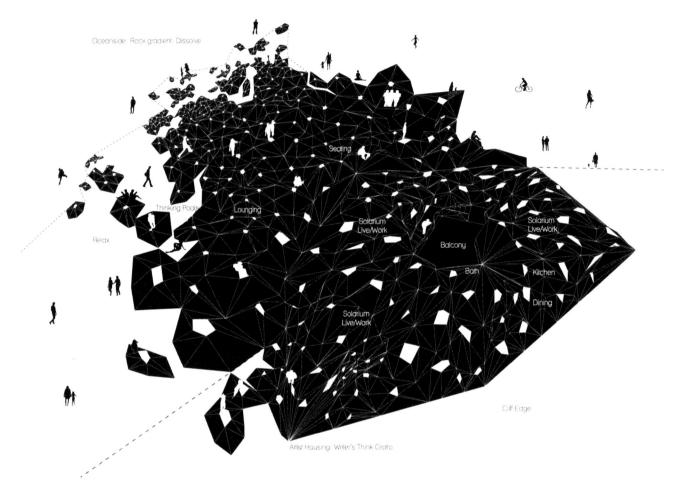

Oceanside · Rock gradient· Dissolve

Seating

Thinking Pools

Lounging

Solarium
Live/Work

Solarium
Live/Work

Relax

Balcony

Bath

Kitchen

Dining

Solarium
Live/Work

Cliff Edge

Artist Housing· Writer's Think Grotto

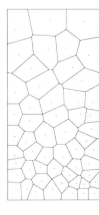
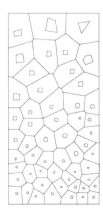

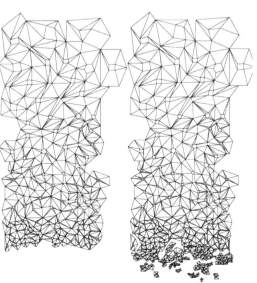

**Malik Benjamin
Megalopolis**

This studio examines the life cycle of global cities along the lines of production, speculative investment, community divestment and urban deterioration. Research begins with 1850's Chicago, includes a trip to Chicago, and concludes with an analysis of Miami - a multi-centered, sprawling medley of nature, building and agriculture with pockets of nuanced social, cultural and political hierarchies. Design projects are founded on network and conduit theory from Jan Gehl, Rodolphe el-Khoury and Charles Landry. It is also influenced by conversations around commerce, innovation and culture from Saskia Sassen, Brad Feld, and William Cronon. The end result is a collection of works covering projects in low speculation areas near global cities.

Jesus Vega

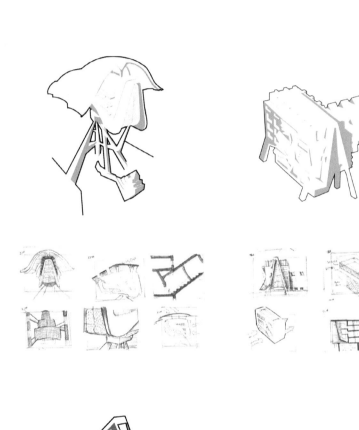

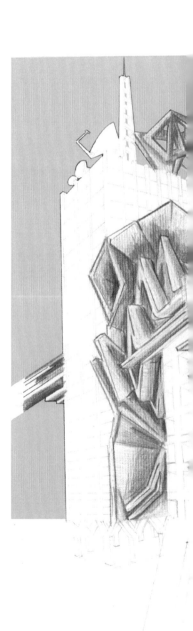

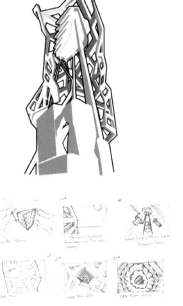

Selene Varela

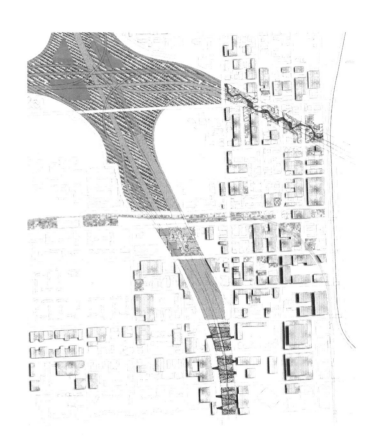

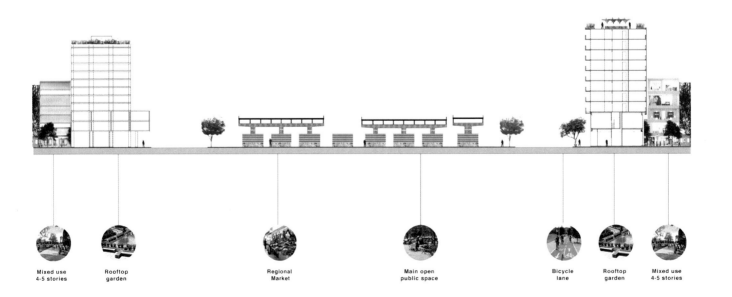

Mixed use
4-5 stories

Rooftop
garden

Regional
Market

Main open
public space

Bicycle
lane

Rooftop
garden

Mixed use
4-5 stories

Jaime Canaves
The Future Transition of the
Guantanamo Naval Base

Since the Fall of 2014, Bermello Ajamil and Partners has been collaborating with our studios, in overseeing and guiding this Master Project design studio. This objective of this course has been to study The Future of Transition of the Guantanamo Naval Base.

The premise of this course envisions a post-Castro Cuba, where there is a free and democratic form of government with human rights and property rights. Furthermore, the course assumes that the Department of Defense and the US Navy have decided under these conditions to demilitarize the base, and that they have provided for public-private partnerships to develop the land for civilian purposes. This is similar to other initiatives in which the Department of Defense has closed military bases for redevelopment by the private sector.

Esther Monterrey

0   75'   150'

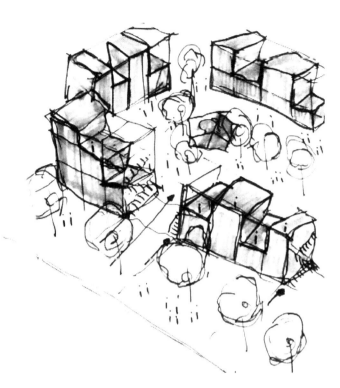

Jaime Vado

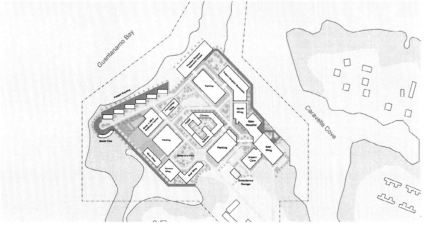

**Eric Goldemberg
Feedback >> Infra-urban
Structure of Networks**

This studio researches network systems in their many different scales, across disciplines. Morphologies are derived from the analysis, diagramming and regeneration of networks configurations to be tested for potential spatial and tectonic pursuits, in order to incorporate the research and production of proto- networks, as part of the foundation research for the thesis.

Understanding the way in which networks are deeply embedded in society and how they are virtually present through enhanced communications systems leads to the formulation of a "network sensibility" that seeks to generate architectural expressions charged with the intelligence, aesthetic and spatial qualities of networks.

Carolina Papale

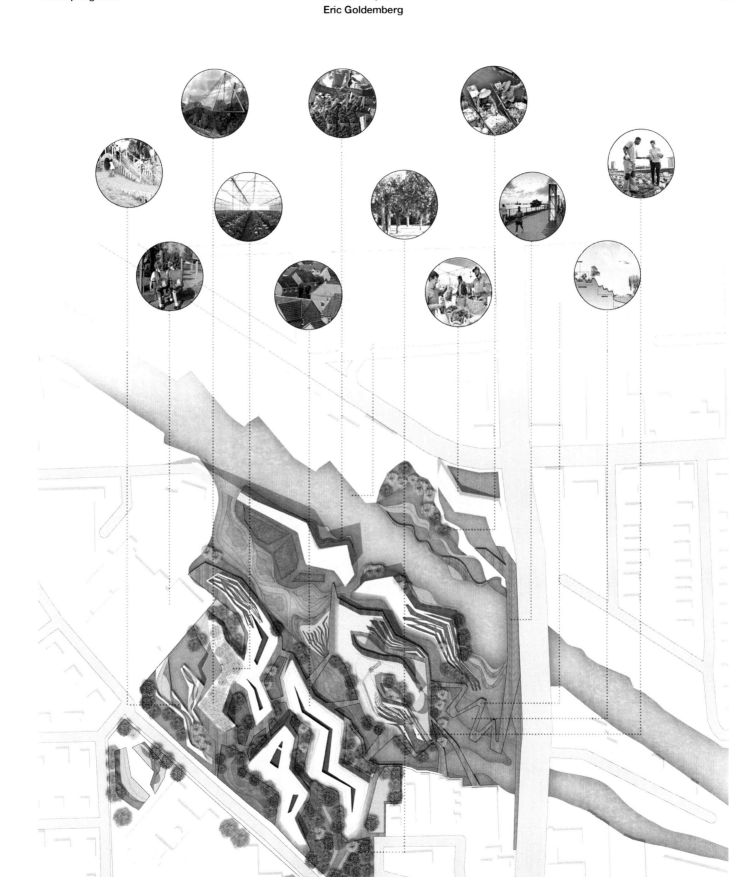

Hassan Sarfraz

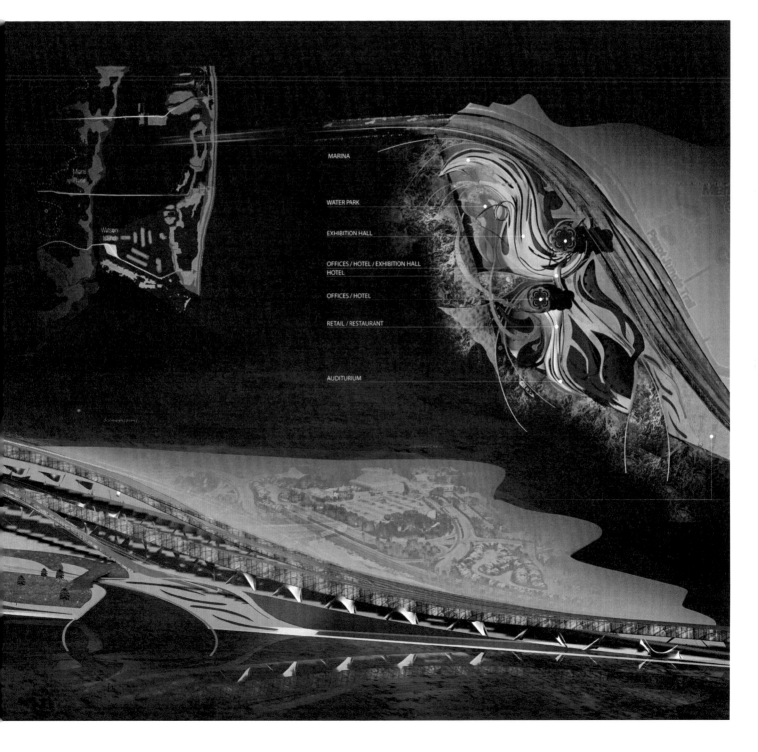

Marilys Nepomechie
Miami + Beach 2100

This Master Project studio asks students to develop phased strategies for urban resilience in Miami and Miami Beach, over the course of the coming century. Studies are carried out in the context of predicted levels of permanent inundation as a result of sea level rise. Based on research completed in the Fall semester, in conjunction with the production of the eponymous exhibition at the Coral Gables Museum, students explore a broad range of approaches to the challenges posed by low elevation, a high water table, a porous substrate, and a sprawling urbanized territory developed between fragile ecosystems.

Among the proposals are: a more compact, higher density Miami - one that is well served by a robust system of elevated public rail and water transit and gradually abandons the automobile; elevated walks, bridges, bicycle lanes and public spaces; wettable buildings and plazas (both newly constructed and retrofitted existing structures); raised and re-imagined historic districts; vertical and floating urban farms; new urban archipelagos - created before flooding begins, but ready to respond to inundation whenever it occurs.

The proposals of artificial deltas and engineered canals, new typologies for buildings, public spaces and infrastructure, and a new public realm in which nature and urbanization are more thoroughly intertwined have proponents among the students' projects. Floating buildings are also among the proposals, as well as entire floating urban blocks - constructed before flooding begins, and ready to become buoyant when inundation occurs. These would become the "ground" for a new generation of Miami real estate development - and would be serviced by flexible infrastructures, both soft and hard.

Taken as a whole, these are visions in which the robust infrastructures of inter-connection are understood to be critical components for a thriving urbanism. Inspired by Dutch "room for the river" strategies, most of the studio proposals are hybrids of man-made and natural systems. Without exception, they explore ways to revisit and profoundly re-imagine the audacious engineering project that first created Miami a century ago.

Crismary Pascarella

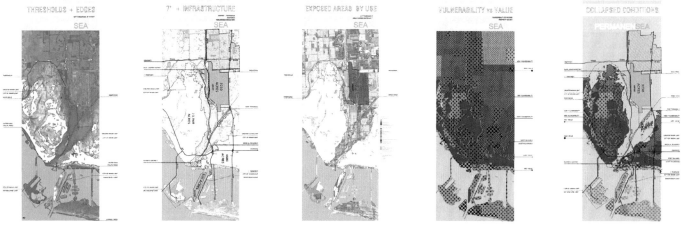

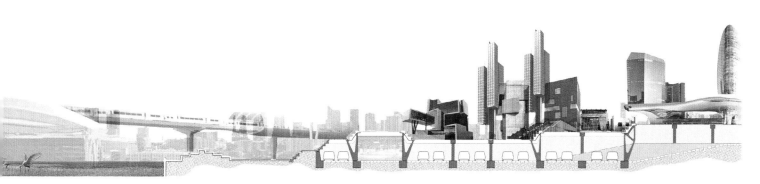

Aileen Zeigen

Eric Peterson
Full-scale Architectural Detail

For more than ten thousand years we have been building things. Some of the oldest known written word deals with the construction of buildings. As designers, what can the things that we want to build tell us about our own ambitions and desires to enter into this ten-thousand-year-old discussion?

The studio course centers around three primary activities: reading, discussing, and making full-scale architectural details. We have read a series of essays, chapters, and selections from pieces of text loosely associated with phenomenology. In the discussions we have attempted to relate ideas from the readings to our own critical practice as designers and active agents in the production of physical culture. We have used reading and design work to explore our own means of approaching the meta-project that is sometimes called civilization, urbanity, culture, or humanity. Ultimately, our aim is to begin to know where we stand in relation to this larger project.

Each student has proposed an architectural detail that is part of a wall and has built it at full scale. Typical programs include a means of passage, a means of viewing out, a means of viewing in, a means of sitting or resting, a means of working, a means of rising up – i.e. a door, a window, a seat, a desk, a stair. The architectural detail should be justified with careful excerpts from specific texts. Final proposals include both architectural drawings and a written discussion of how the ideas expressed through architectural detail are related to those texts.

Ludovico Ferro

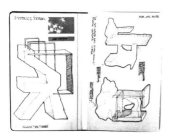
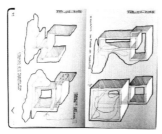
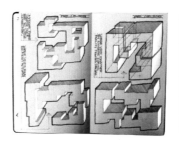
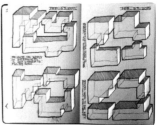

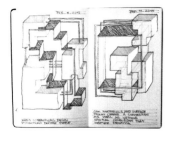
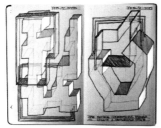
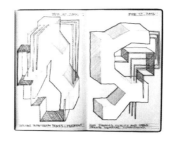
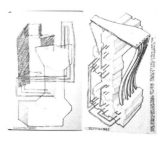

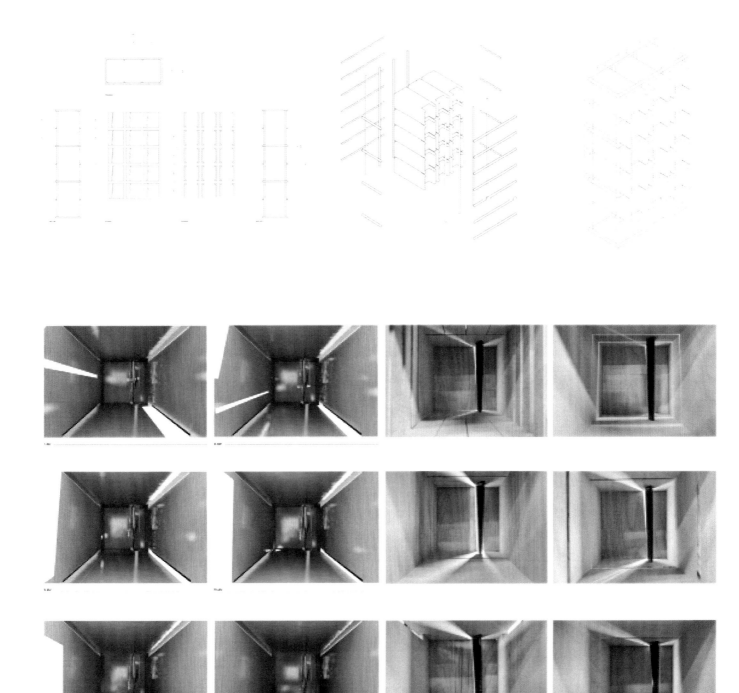

Eileen Nunes

Camilo Rosales
Innovative Tectonics

This Masters Project has multiple programs, since each student has selected his/ her own project and site. What unites the effort is the notion that personal values ultimately drive design decisions. Students were encouraged to rigorously clarify their own preferences and to formulate design concepts based on them. The studio contemplates well developed solutions at a variety of scales including site planning, urban or suburban implications, and innovative tectonics. A variety of presentation techniques will be explored ranging from sketch models to digital graphics and fabrications.

Anabel Mendt Ehrman

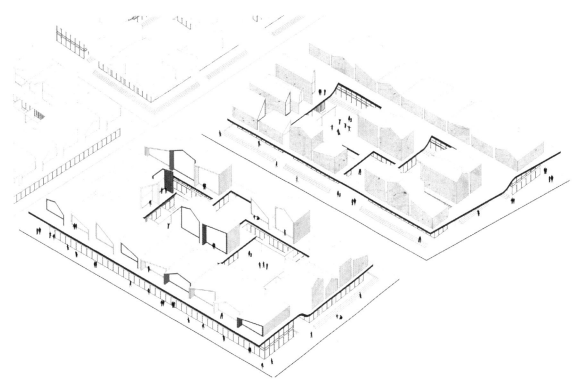

Dina Karimullina

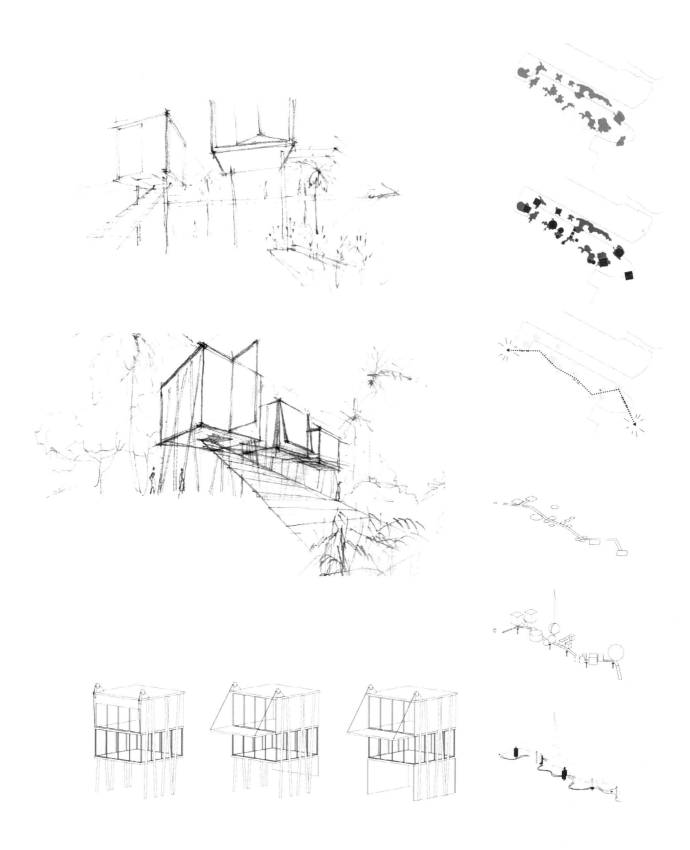

Miami
Matters
One

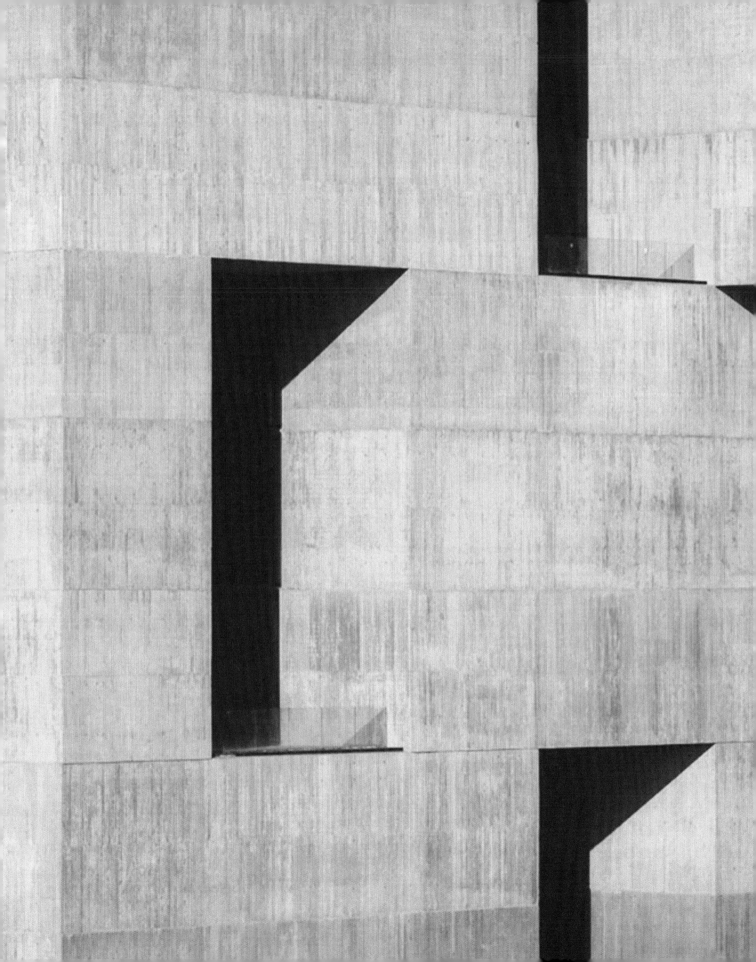

Juan Ignacio Cerda
Elisa Silva

Folio
Adam Bierman
Jennifer Kramer
Larissa Marenco
Marny Pereda
Amaru Rios
Henry Rueda

Excerpt from an interview with Juan Ignacio Cerda
from Elemental Arquitectura and Elisa Silva from
Enlace Arquitectura

Juan Ignacio Cerda -JIC-
Elemental Arquitectura, Santiago Chile

Our strength is the search for innovation and design in projects of public interest and social impact, for which we count on a team highly enabled in the development of complex initiatives that require coordination of public and private actors alongside participatory processes for decision-making. We see the city as a powerful instrument that has the potential to create wealth and can act as a medium through which we can generate quality of life. Therefore, we understand the projects we develop—housing, infrastructure, transportation, institutional buildings and public spaces—as opportunities to extend the benefits of the city to all.

Elisa Silva -ES-
Enlace Arquitectura, Caracas Venezuela

The office focuses on projects related to sustainable architecture, urban design, landscape architecture and slum upgrading, as well as research and publications. Enlace has been awarded in several competitions including first prize in the Rehabilitation of Sabana Grande Boulevard Competition in 2008. The built Pavement project for Sabana Grande won the VIII Bienal Iberoamericana de Arquitectura y Urbanismo in 2012. Enlace received first prize in the Maracay Metropolitan Park Competition in 2011, which also received first prize for Non Built Projects in the XI National Architecture Bienal 2014. The proposal for the Public Ideas Competition to transform the La Carlota military base into a Green Metropolitan Park 2012 was selected as one of three finalists and received Honorable Mention.

-Folio-

In Miami we have really expensive buildings and we also have socially segregated low income neighborhoods that have been neglected for years. Every city has social differences, but it is very different when cities have slopes and mountains [from] when they are flat. When cities are flat, the segregation become[s] invisible. And when it is so segregated, there's no way that you can mix it unless you do really powerful approaches in design. So, when you work with local communities, do you have any methodologies that could be applied to [the] low income neighborhoods in Miami?

-JIC-

In Miami [there] is a problem of inequality, you are in a rich country but some people [are] not making the most of [the available] assets [for] the city. The only way to solve inequality is [through] education but it is a long-term process. [Meanwhile], we think that [there is a] shortcut to solve inequality in the city. Hernando de Soto, [Peruvian author of "The Mystery of Capital"], talks about [making informal settlements formal]. As soon as you become formal you have an asset. That asset can be used [towards a] mortgage, inheritance for your kids, education, or [even to expanding] your small business. [However,] in Miami I imagine that the formal exists, [so] it is not a problem of formal [versus] informal, [but rather] a problem of quality of life in the outskirts of the city. Two things are quite important to [address this] problem. [The] first [is] public space in terms of street mix of use, cycle lanes [and] things that may raise the value of your property. The second thing is public [transportation], meaning, connect[ing] the people to the city and the city to the people.

-ES-

In terms of social inclusion, these are the three key issues: connectivity, access to public space and capacity building which can either be education or that you are able to meet the jobs that are available in that moment in the market. And there is also another point that we talk about a lot is integrating different offices within the city to be able to have more resources funneled in an accurate way and not dispersed between isolated transportation projects or isolated streetscape improvement projects. And that's a difficult task in terms of organization but the potential of it having a very lasting impression is much [larger].

-Folio-

Appreciate that both of you have a sensibility to nature and [design to] join architecture with the environment around. In a city, [such as Miami], that is quickly densifying and is run by developers, who do not have the same interests [architects] do, how do you tackle that challenge [of designing transition spaces between interior and exterior and also make the most of natural resources]? [For instance, the PAMM] is one of the few buildings that we have like this [in Miami], but if you look down the street, most of them are condominiums that do not have that integration.

-ES-

That is a good question and a partial answer is the fact that somehow in the United States, development has progressed outside of the profession of architecture. Development is of course inspired and motivated by different priorities such as the square meters of space that you are able to consolidate and sell. [However], some of these [transition] spaces are not an amenity that you can put a price on or sell, they are not quantifiable. Within these development paradigms, [such spaces are] a waste if you judge it within those frameworks. So, I would not say that [developers] are not interested in these strategies, but they are not rewarded for them. It would be very interesting for schools, such as FIU, to get the developers' attention and try to find what produces models that are less environmentally friendly, and perhaps with the city, find other strategies that could be well worth pursuing.

-JIC-

I really agree with Elisa, [and] I would like to add another thing that relates to the teaching of architecture. The problem of [convincing] developers is at the same [time] a problem [with] architects. We have become irrelevant in our exercise of the profession. We are not able to discuss with a developer because we do not know how to discuss with them. Developers have restrictions [and] conditions [to run] their business and we have to deal with them as well. So, for [me], developers are not a problem, the problem are architects who have not faced real problems in their careers. [Also], this is happening in architecture schools that [teach] things that are not relevant for the exercise of the profession. So, if we have the courage to challenge [some of] those topics, work with restrictions, and use design to convince [developers that it is possible to] have spaces that you can sell, you [will] have nice architecture.

Design Ten

Marilys Nepomech

Alice Cimring

Malik Benjamin

Nick Gelpi

Miguel Peguero

FRESH KUT BARBER SHOP UNISEX

Nanette Martinez / Haley Perry
Sharzad Mirshahidi / Hassan Sarfraz
Esther Monterrey / Jacqueline Rowe

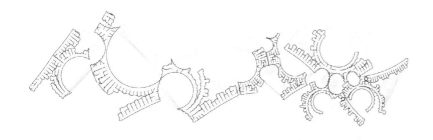

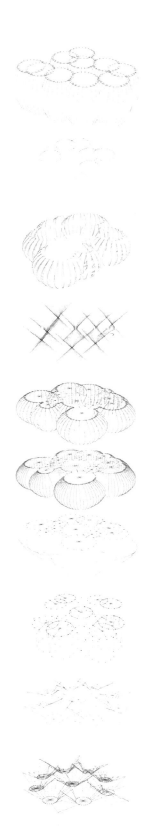

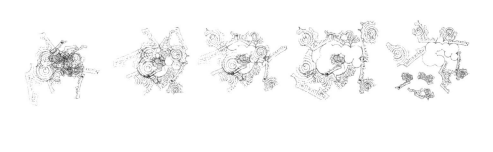

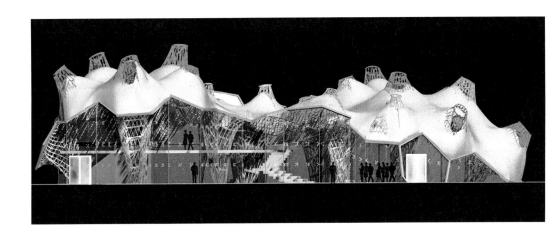

Ludovico Ferro
Jaime Vado
Kevin Vildosola

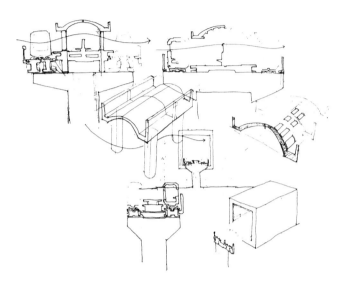
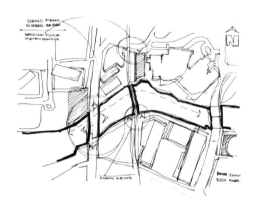

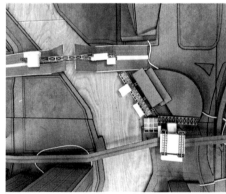

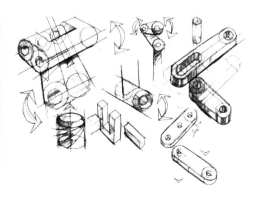

Design 10
Marilys Nepomechie

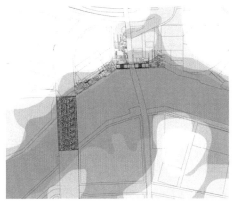

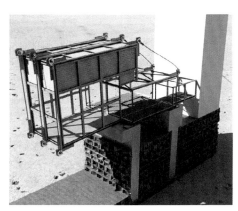

Design Nine

Thomas Spiegelha

Gray Read *Co-Co*

Claudia Busch

Jordan Trachtenb

Henry Rueda

Sabah Corso

Adrian Heid

Claudio Salazar

ter *Coordinator*
rdinator

rg

Mark Miglionico / Adriana Marie Rojas
David Ciambotti
Jennifer Kramer

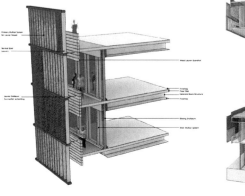

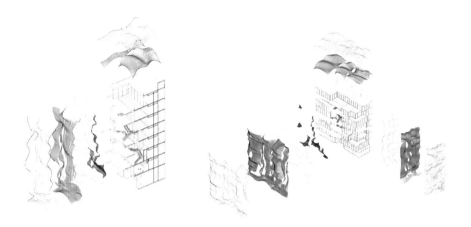

Catherine Pageau
Claudia Fernandez
Michael Lassandro

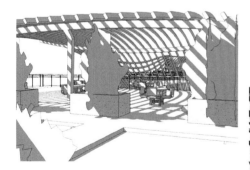

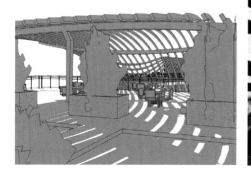

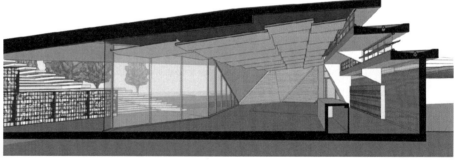

DiGiacomo / Alzate / Rojas
Wasala / Galvan / Romero
Rogers / Miskowiec / Shapiro

Thomas Spiegelhalter
Claudia Busch

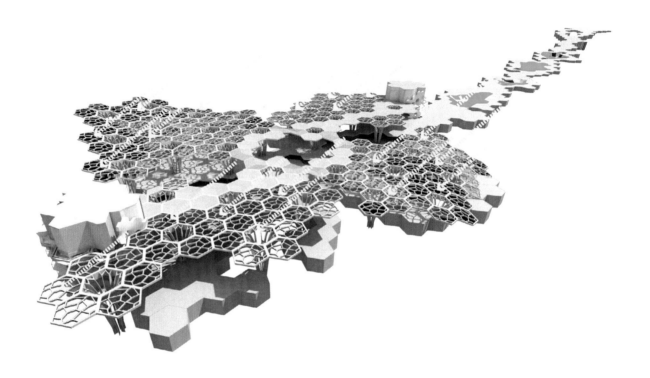

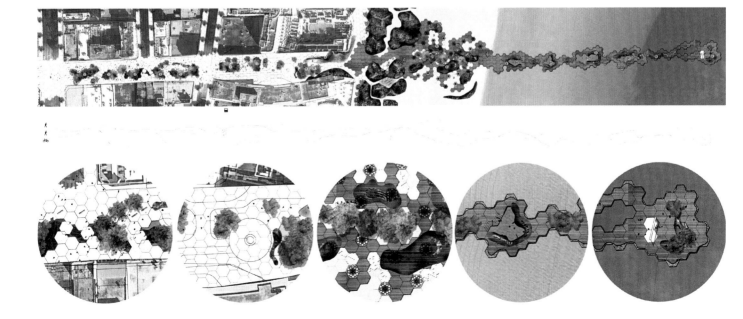

Miami
Matters

Margi Nothard

Folio
Larissa Marenco
Adam Bierman
Jason Chandler
Henry Rueda

Images
Robin Hill

The context of Miami is particularly deficient in addressing affordable housing. There are images of two worlds, the world of the high-end condo and the separated, taxed, single-family house. They are both models of privacy/disengagement; neither engages the city.

Glavovic Studio

Founded in 1999, Glavovic Studio Inc. is an award-winning design firm located in South Florida. Glavovic Studio explores and produces contemporary architecture, art and urban design, focusing on exceptional creative processes and client oriented services that engage the environment and provide social value.

Excerpt from an interview with Margi Nothard -MN-, principal of Glavovic Studio

-Folio-
How do you see social housing? Are there any changes in the way people view it in Miami? Do you see any improvement?

-MN-
I feel that there is a lot of housing coming to the fore, developers are starting to propose affordable housing projects, and it's not at the scale that we need, it's just not good enough. It's that sort of housing where it meets the minimum needs, only. There is a list of state and federal requirements for such housing and you can check each of the items on the list, and still actually not do good housing.
And so, what we have to do is re-write the program on a set of different terms. And, if you do that, and anyone can do that, really, it's a paradigm shift.

-Folio-
Why would you choose to embrace the difficult road you've chosen?

-MN-
Why we do affordable housing? It's really just a fundamental problem to solve. I don't have any other motivation just that it's essential and it must be done. We take it on as both an urban challenge and an environmental challenge. We also try to think of it as the most value-engineered proposition right at the get go, if you had to take away everything that's what the design has to be at the beginning and that's how we get through the process. In Kennedy Homes people drive by and they want to go and live there, and they're not the people with the lowest incomes in the community.

-Folio-
How do you do that on a budget though? That's a remarkable thing.

-MN-
It's not really. Kennedy Homes is $92 a square foot including all the land and everything. Some facts about Kennedy Homes… eight

and a half acres, 11 buildings, so its harder because you have a lot of surface area and many different types of buildings: two five-story buildings, three three-story buildings, three two-story buildings, three adaptive-use buildings…

We basically designed the buildings around a 24 foot wide modular unit, and it's either a one bedroom and it gets slightly longer for a two bedroom or three bedroom.

That module allows us to then do two different designs: it's either a single noted corridor or it's a pinwheel. The whole building is very environmentally responsive and allows you to create these micro courtyards and creates this very sensitive cross ventilation of air so there are spaces where people can gather.

-Folio-
We know you are working on other projects now that involve a real sensitivity to the existing community. Is that part of your process now, where you say not just "we are going to create an environment for living", but "we are also really going to be doing our research and think about this on some level beyond what usually happens"?

-MN-
We know you are working on other projects now that involve a real sensitivity to the existing community. Is that part of your process now, where you say not just "we are going to create an environment for living", but "we are also really going to be doing our research and think about this on some level beyond what usually happens"?

-Folio-
You do what many people describe as Activist Architecture, most obviously with your work on socially significant projects. Are there other, less obvious, ways in which you engage the community?

-MN-
We do that in a number of ways. For example, we hold a free public forum once a month at our studio at which we host guest lecturers. FIU's own David Rifkind was a guest lecturer there. During the controversial times surrounding the discourse about Kennedy Homes, we invited people who were literally yelling and screaming at us, and we opened up the studio, we made books, we made coffee and tea and cookies, and we invited them to just come and have a roundtable.

-Folio-
The legacy of housing is not necessarily seen the day it opens; it's the long track. The two tracks of affordable housing are (1) it's

attractive enough that it becomes gentrified and people with money move in and it's no longer affordable housing, or (2) it falls to wrack and ruin and becomes a problem. How does the architect respond to this?

-MN-
Well, there are a couple of different ways of dealing with this. On the Kennedy Homes, there is a 99-year HUD lease, which makes it very difficult to change its use. Also, on this site, 20 percent of the units have been reserved for the low- and very low-income levels, there are very specific constraints on who can live there. It's very hard to change these constraints, so it's not likely to get gentrified. It could fall apart if it's not maintained, just as a good quality project could fall apart if it's not maintained. I am very concerned and when I drive by and I feel that they are not cleaning properly, I have raked the leaves.

-Folio-
What did this project reveal to you about being an architect that was something you would never have imagined as a student and also as a practitioner, particularly, what does this project tell you about the practice of architecture?

-MN-
We did a special event after finishing the project, hosted it at one of the project's community centers, and invited the residents; one of the residents spoke about how this project had changed his life. Everyone was quiet. It was so moving because he just said he would never have imagined that he would live in such a beautiful place. He spoke about how his family, when they visit, they now know that he is a successful person.

-Folio-
…Dignity

-MN-
That, for me, was a moment I knew that whatever we'd done made sense.

-Folio-
What was the lesson?

-MN-
The lesson learned was that this is about creating environments that are contributing, that this is something that I can actually do.

Design Comprehe

Henry Rueda Coo.
Mark Marine
Claudia Busch
Michael Repovich

sive

dinator

David Ciambotti
Pedro Lenartowicz
Valentina Garibello

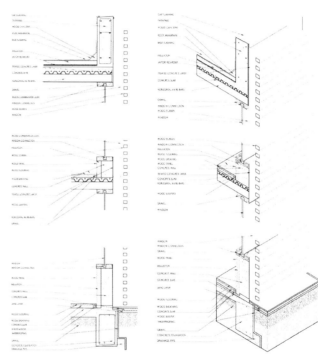

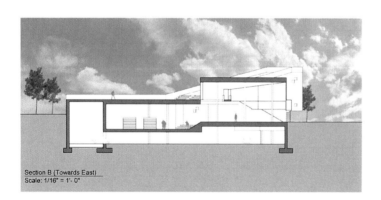

Section B (Towards East)
Scale: 1/16" = 1'- 0"

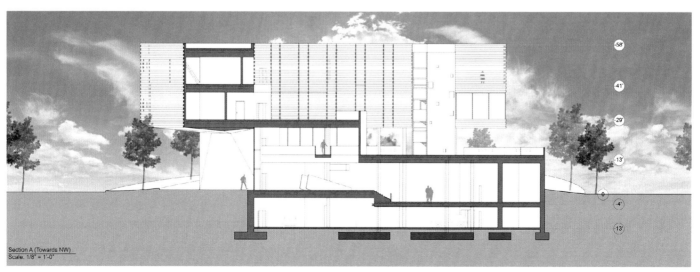

Section A (Towards NW)
Scale: 1/8" = 1'-0"

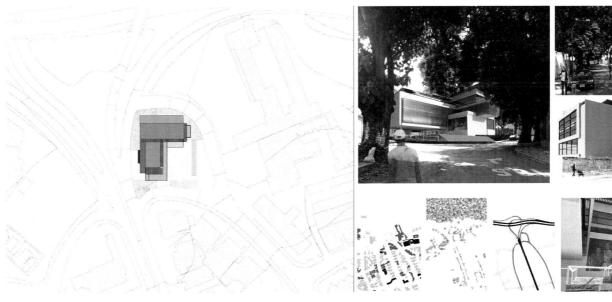

Michael Flores

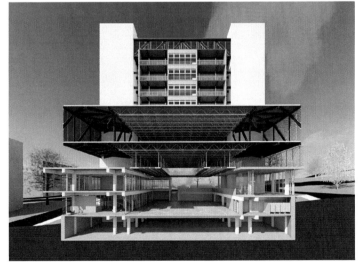

Ariel Gonzalez
Crismary Pascarella

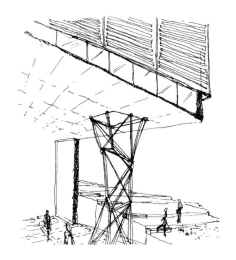

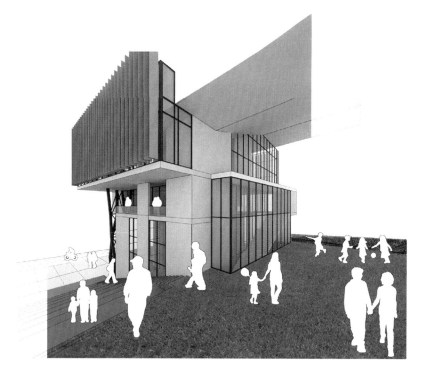

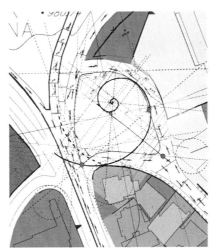

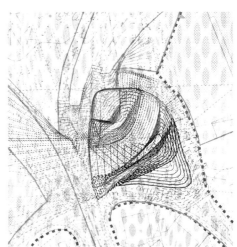

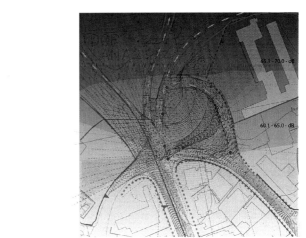

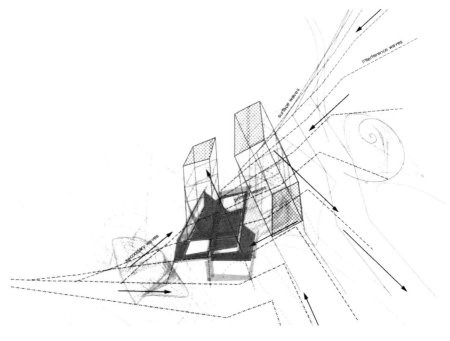

Catherine Pageau

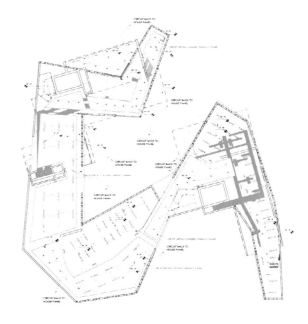

Kevin Tenor
Kevin Vildosola

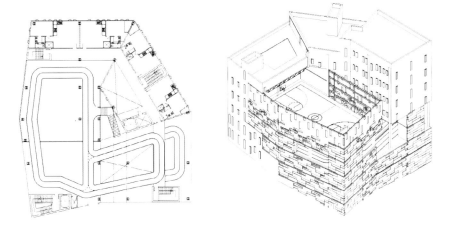

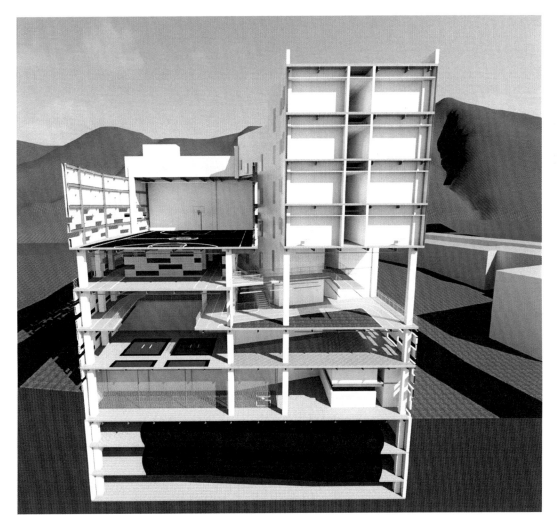

Design Eight
Jaime Canaves
Thomas Spiegelha
Eric Goldemberg
Alfredo Andia
Camilo Rosales
Diego Camargo

ter

Valeria Fossi
Giovanna Gallardo Pinera
Carlos Gener
Paula Montealegre
Julia Sarduy

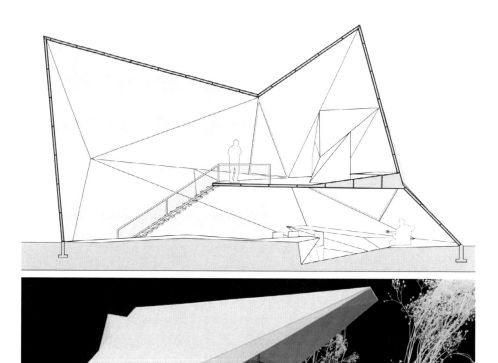

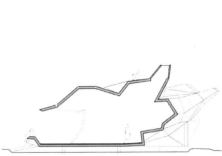

Stephany Guinan
Zoe Russian Moreno
Naaly Pierre

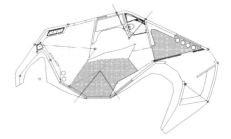

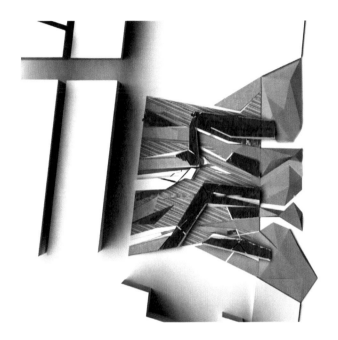

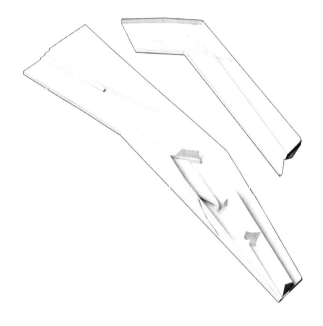

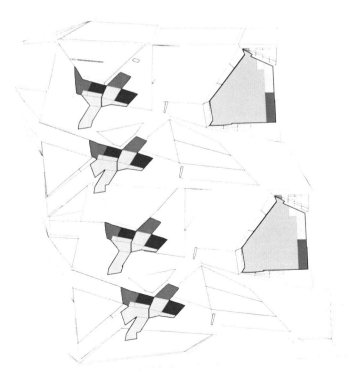

Albert Elias
Maria Sol Rivera
Leonardo Montalban

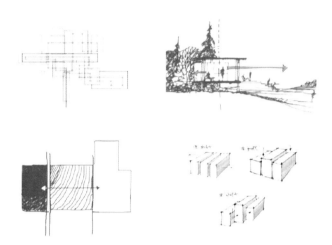

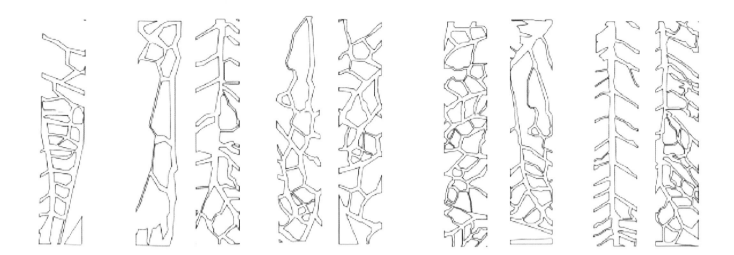

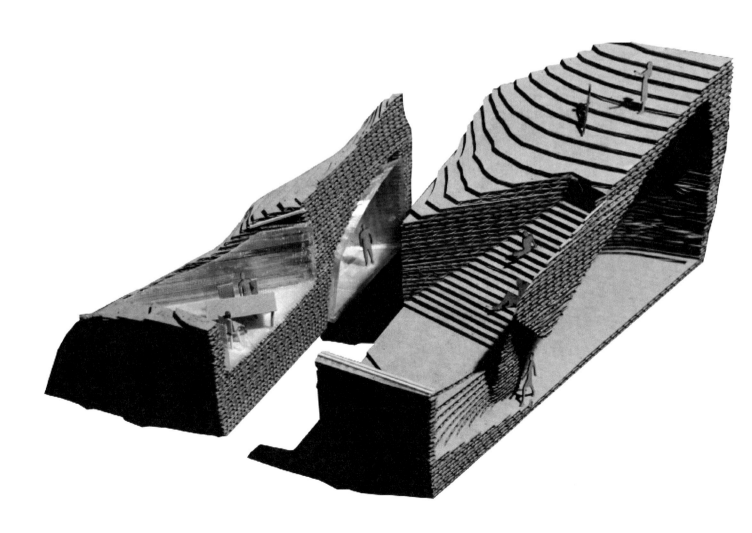

Shane Batchelor
Nelly Salgueiro
Anette Nolasco

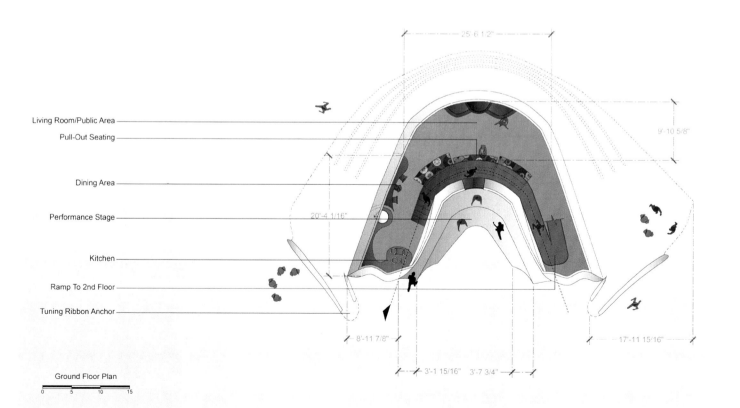

Living Room/Public Area
Pull-Out Seating
Dining Area
Performance Stage
Kitchen
Ramp To 2nd Floor
Tuning Ribbon Anchor

25'-6 1/2"
9'-10 5/8"
20'-4 1/16"
8'-11 7/8"
3'-1 15/16"   3'-7 3/4"
17'-11 15/16"

Ground Floor Plan

0   5   10   15

Design Seven / Ei

Jason Chandler
and Adam Drisin

Folio Summer 2014

Design 7 / 8
Jason Chandler
Adam Drisin

ARC 5340

102

Felicito Rodriguez
Pedro Lenartowicz

Folio Summer 2014

Design 7 / 8
Jason Chandler
Adam Drisin

ARC 5340

103

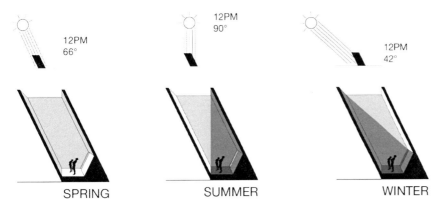

12PM
66°

12PM
90°

12PM
42°

SPRING   SUMMER   WINTER

Design Six / Form

Jason Chandler C

Glenda Puente

Nathaly Haratz

Armando Rigau

Adam Drisin

Cynthia Ottchen

tive Two
ordinator

Joshua Perez
Fernando Salcedo
Juan Manuel Gatica

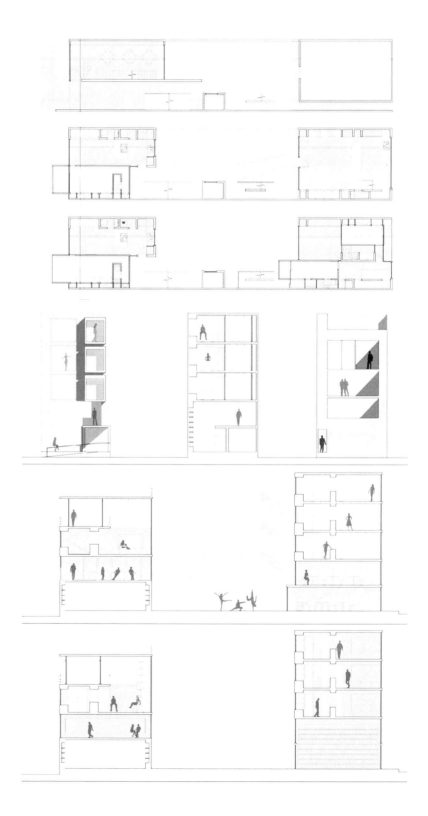

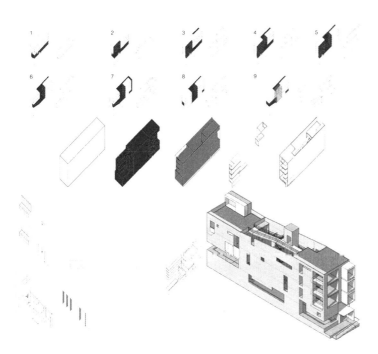

Vikki Tou Li
Jorge Camelo
Christopher Gongora

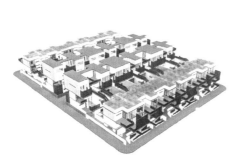

Miami
Matters

Manuel Clavel Rojo

Folio
Luca de Giacomo
Pedro Lenartowicz
Byron Muñoz
Glenn Muñoz
Mario Ortiz
Catherine Pageau
Felicito Rodriguez
Henry Rueda

Images
David Frutos

Excerpt from an interview
with Manuel Clavel Rojo -MCR-

-Folio-
Manuel, you have had the opportunity to work in your native Spain, as well as in China and the Middle East and miami; How does Miami's institutional system compare to the rest?

-MCR-
In terms of social inclusion, these are the three key issues: connectivity, access to public space and capacity building which can either be education or that you are able to meet the jobs that are available in that moment in the market. And there is also another point that we talk about a lot is integrating different offices within the city to be able to have more resources funneled in an accurate way and not dispersed between isolated transportation projects or isolated streetscape improvement projects. And that's a difficult task in terms of organization but the potential of it having a very lasting impression is much [larger].

-Folio-
Although, it may be that cities like Miami and Miami Beach are the only examples in the country of this transformation because they are places that are totally open to immigrants and the innovation they may bring.

-MCR-
Absolutely, if you go to a city like Weston or Coral Gables of course it is terrible. It is fun to hear people still talk in Coral Gables about the 'Spanish Style', I am from Spain and that's not the 'Spanish Style', don't tell me it's Spanish because you invented that a few years ago, and you should stop. I agree there are some things you have to take care of. Look I come from a city that was founded something like one thousand five hundred years ago, so I know what the deal is with history, and its good to keep history. I worked on a reconstruction and we found a small statue of the Virgin in one corner, and because our projects are very public there was a lot of talk on the blogs about the future of the this image. One commenter wrote that the Virgin had been in that building for five hundred years—that's the weight of history in our city—the comment went on to say: "I'm sure this guys are going to destroy the image". I was not planning to do it and while it was an issue for the developer at the end everyone was convinced so the Virgin was kept and it was very successful. Sometimes it's very easy to respect these traditions while being innovative in other areas.

-Folio-
Your practice requires that you work with different countries and institutions. How do you do it?

-MCR-
You always have to partner. I would say that most of the issues I have had were due to not having the right partner.

-Folio-
How do you go about finding the right partner?

-MCR-
You are always able to call someone and ask for two or three names and you create a network. When I work here in Miami I always partner with a licensed architect.

Of course there is also the issue of cultural differences, which can become a problem. Sometimes it can be worse if you speak the same language. For example, in Mexico the word ahorita could mean now, of course ahorita could also mean not now, but forget about it! It is known that in China they never say no so you need a partner that can help you control this cultural issues.

-Folio-
How much of the place do you take into account? Do you accept input from the local architect?

-MCR-
Of course, you have to do it. Otherwise, it becomes a very complicated situation where you are designing things that in the end are not possible to build. There are general concepts in architecture that work well here or there, but there are other more specific things like regulations due to hurricanes in Miami. Windows have to be certain sizes; they have to be hurricane protected, very expensive. Of course, it's good to have regulations but without it being something crazy. In the Design District, we have a building with cars on the façade and someone wanted to make a hurricane proof test for the car—the car runs 200 km per hour, what else do you want! That kind of crazy thing is frustrating but you are paid to not be frustrated so you don't do it.

-Folio-
Can you tell us a little about how you see the approach to architectural education in different countries like Spain and the US? And also, what kind of professionals come out from those educational systems.

-MCR-
There is a very different relationship between the teacher and the student in the states, at least in certain universities, than in other countries. Although, I would say that Spain is now more and more similar to the states, in the bad sense, because if you want to regulate everything to the point where a teacher is scared to get sued for putting a lot of pressure on the student, the education process suffers.

What's most interesting for me and for my students is to understand that you can give many different solutions to one problem. So if you have one hundred students, you have one hundred visions, one hundred analyses, which is the real knowledge: you are learning from you own process but also from the processes of everybody else. You can always have your private lessons, but we should promote bigger size classes because it works for design studios, perhaps not for other classes like structure and history, but that intensity is absolutely amazing for students of architecture.

-Folio-
Miami has become the kind of city where everyone wants to do work, big architecture names want to design here and developers want them here, but there is very little in the way of public projects. How could we change that? How could we create a connection to the public always?

-MCR-
I think the private sector understands that design is good because is really how the market works. I don't think is necessary to have paternalism from the government involved. I always say you have to use a bike because you care about the environment, but also because the bike is practical. So when things are reasonable, they always happen. If everyone in a society understands that design is good—for the developers because they sell better, for the end-user because they have a better life in modern spaces—then they get it. Sometimes, governments try to promote those values through their own buildings, but its good that the private sector understands this by itself.

For me it has been very interesting to be here in Miami because I have seen the transformation of a city, which is trying to think of design as a creative industry that is able to bring income.

Design Five / For

Jason Chandler C

Jordan Trachtenb

Glen Santayana

Cynthia Ottchen

Adrian Heid

Nicholas Baker

Eric Peterson

Elite Kedan

ative One
ordinator
rg

Maria Paglia
Susana Alonso
Lilian Marin Saenz

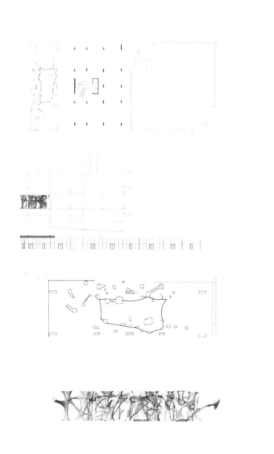

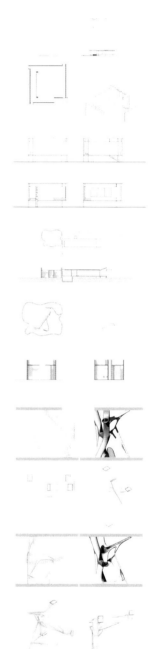

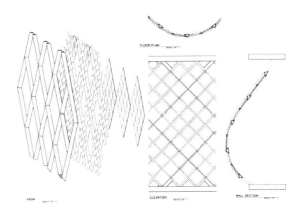

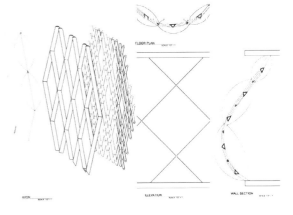

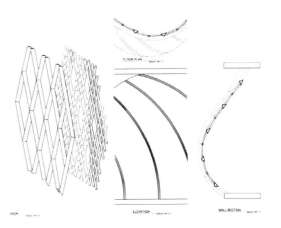

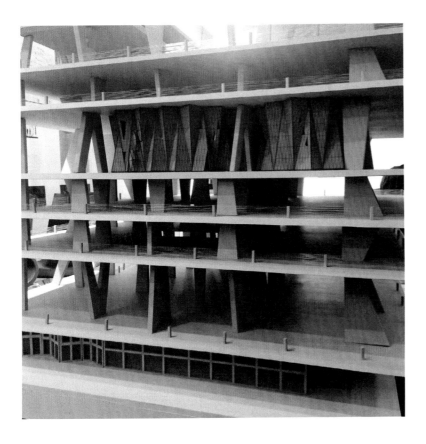

Sharit Ben Asher
Alejandro Diaz

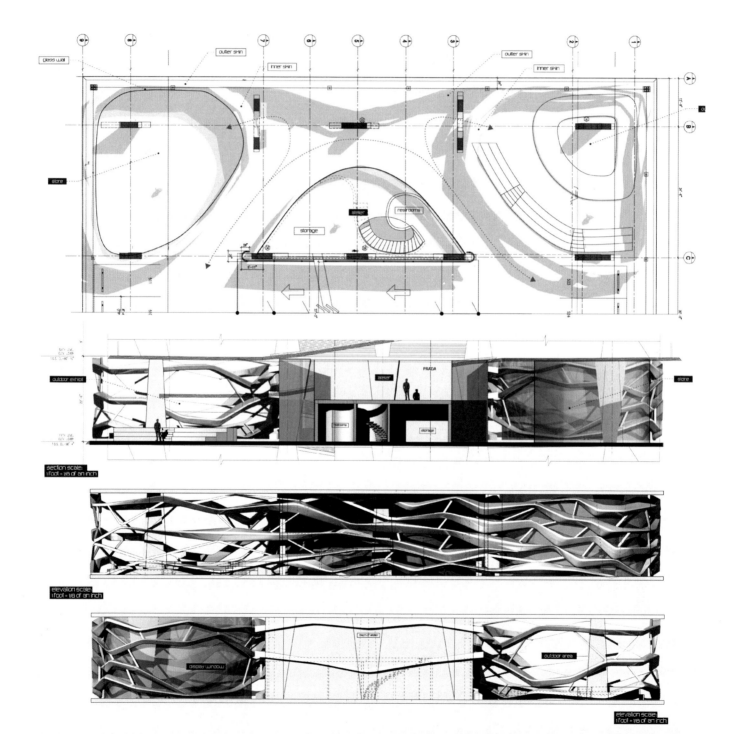

outdoor exhibit

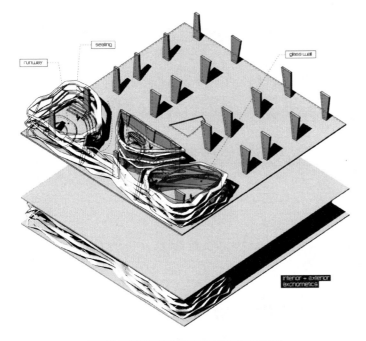

seating

runway

glass wall

interior + exterior axonometrics

elevation scale
1 foot = 1/8 of an inch

John Udbardy
Priscilla Cuadra
Stephania Soltau

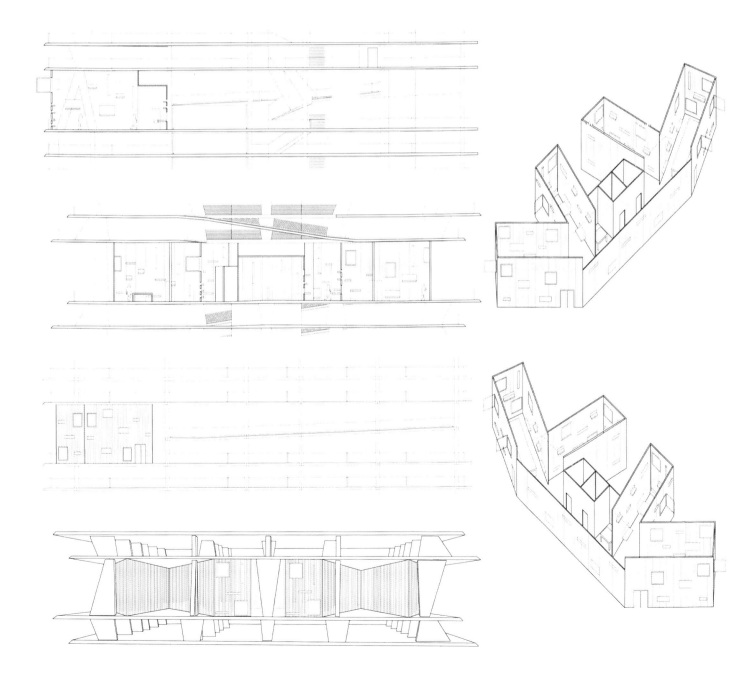

Jessie Cardenas
Yenisley Lopez

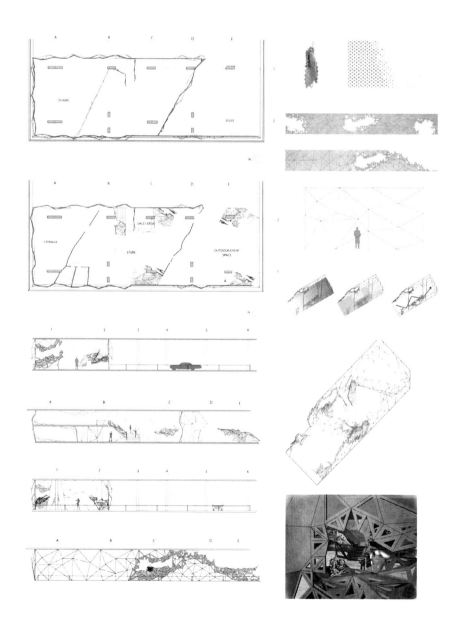

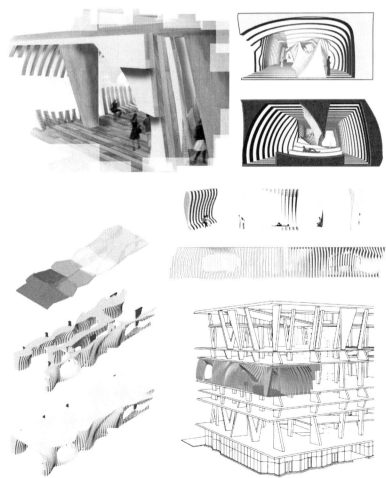

Julia Sarduy
Maria Sol Rivera

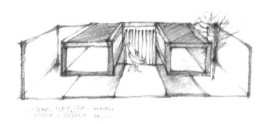

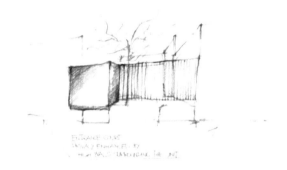

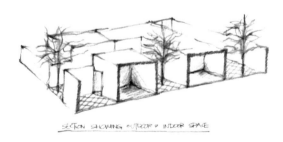

SECTION SHOWING OUTDOOR & INDOOR SPACE

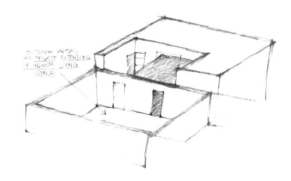

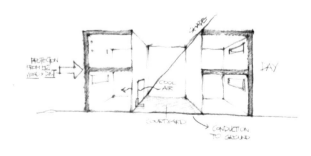

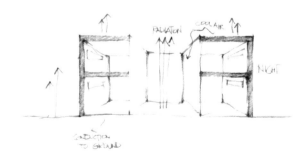

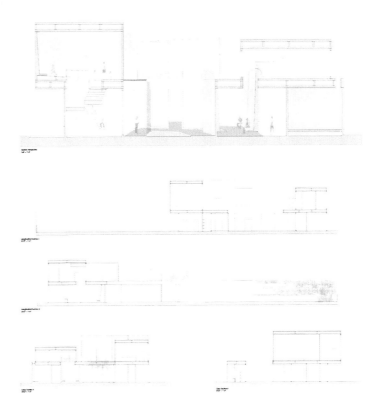

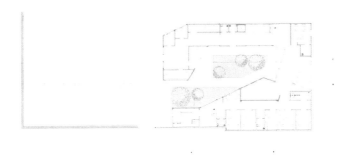

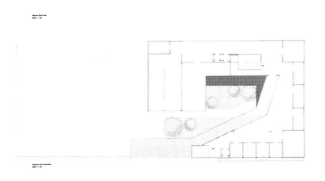

Vivian Contreras Morales
Tyler Reagan

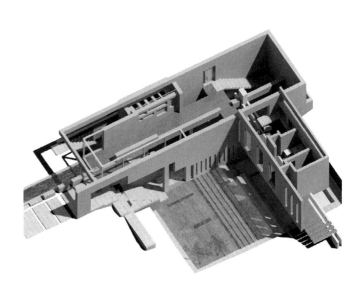

DESIGN CONCEPT
SEQUENCE OF FACTS THROUGH LIGHT...

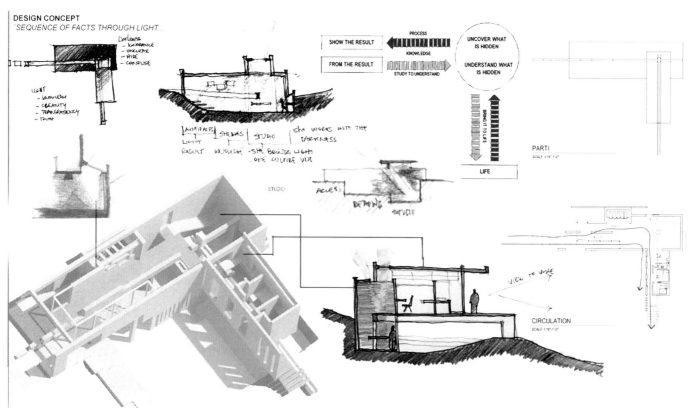

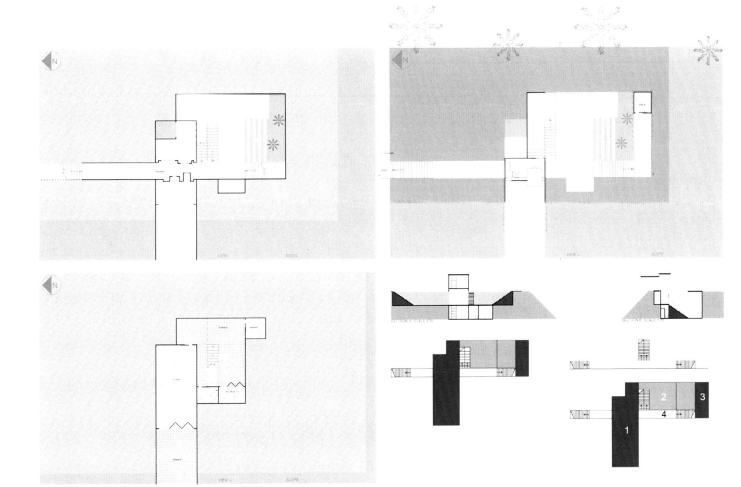

Design Four
Nick Gelpi *Coordi[...]*
Andrea Perelli
Jeff Lodin

ator

Maria Flores
Elise Francis
Daniel de la Cruz

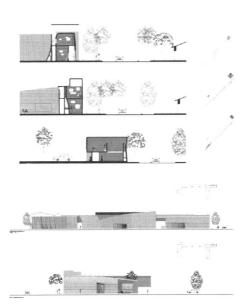

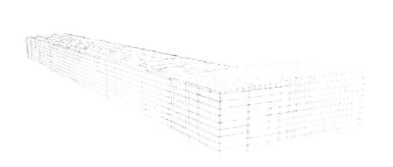

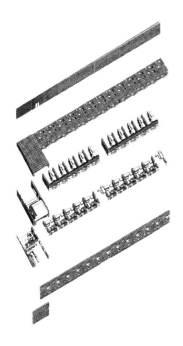

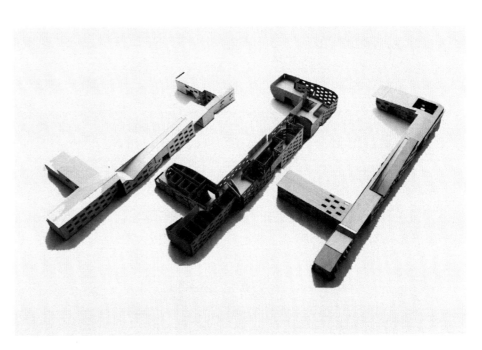

Maria Paula Soler
Andres Barros

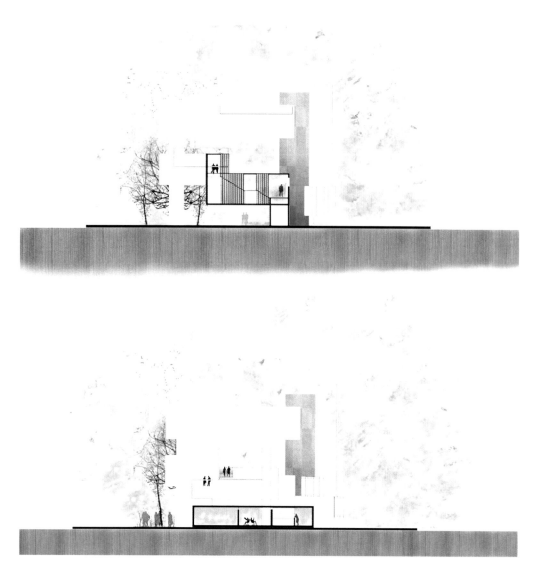

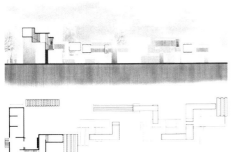

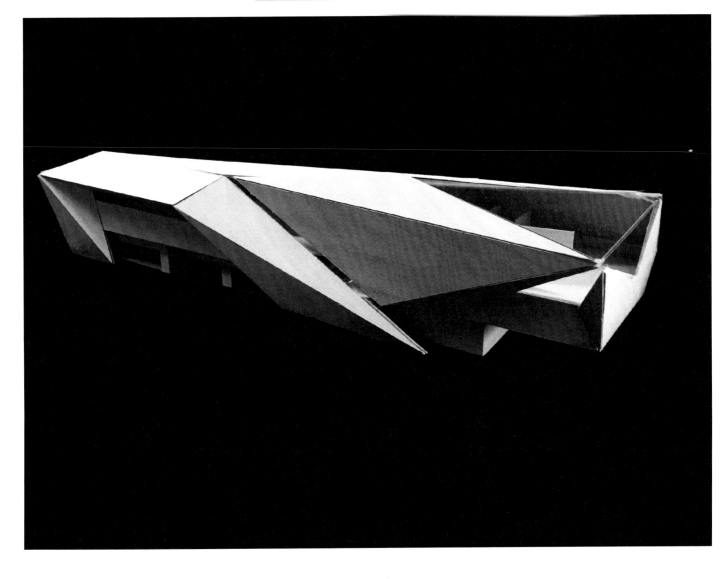

Design Three
Eric Peterson Coo
Patrick Soares
Felice Grodin

dinator

Adriana Balcaceres
Maria Flores
Mack Dominic

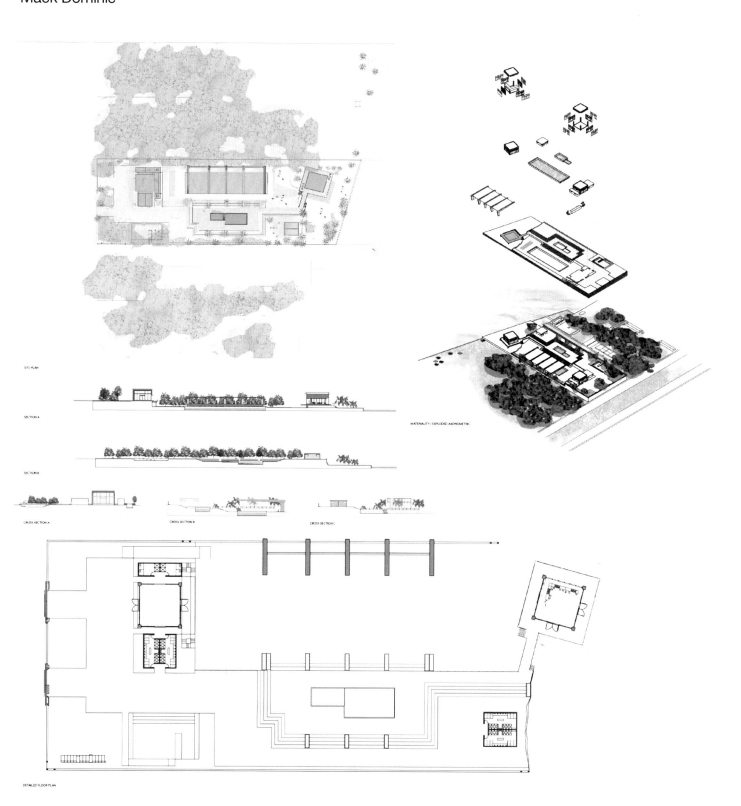

SITE PLAN

SECTION A

SECTION B

MATERIALITY / EXPLODED AXONOMETRIC

CROSS SECTION A   CROSS SECTION B   CROSS SECTION C

DETAILED FLOOR PLAN

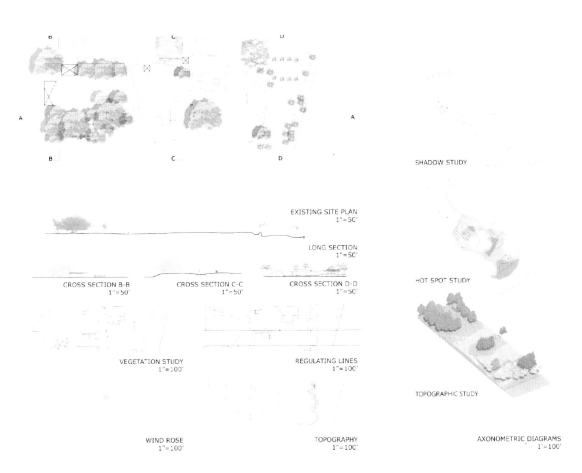

B

C

D

A

A

B

C

D

SHADOW STUDY

EXISTING SITE PLAN
1"=50'

LONG SECTION
1"=50'

HOT SPOT STUDY

CROSS SECTION B-B
1"=50'

CROSS SECTION C-C
1"=50'

CROSS SECTION D-D
1"=50'

VEGETATION STUDY
1"=100'

REGULATING LINES
1"=100'

TOPOGRAPHIC STUDY

WIND ROSE
1"=100'

TOPOGRAPHY
1"=100'

AXONOMETRIC DIAGRAMS
1'=100'

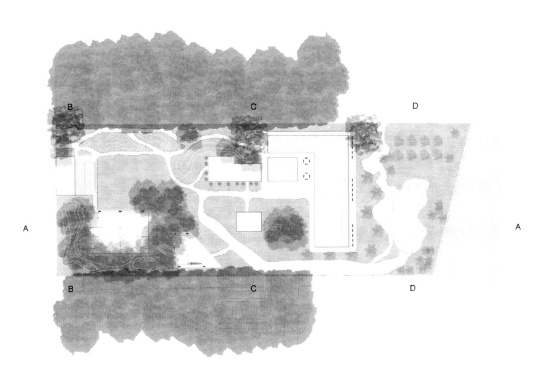

B

C

D

A

A

B

C

D

Alejandra Lopez
Camille Cortes

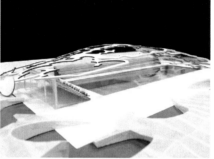

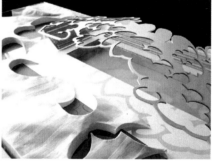

Design Two
Nik Nedev *Coordi*
Jorge Balboa
Marco Campa
Sara Garaulet
Emmanuel Ferro
Elite Kedan
Felice Grodin

ator

Camila Lohezic

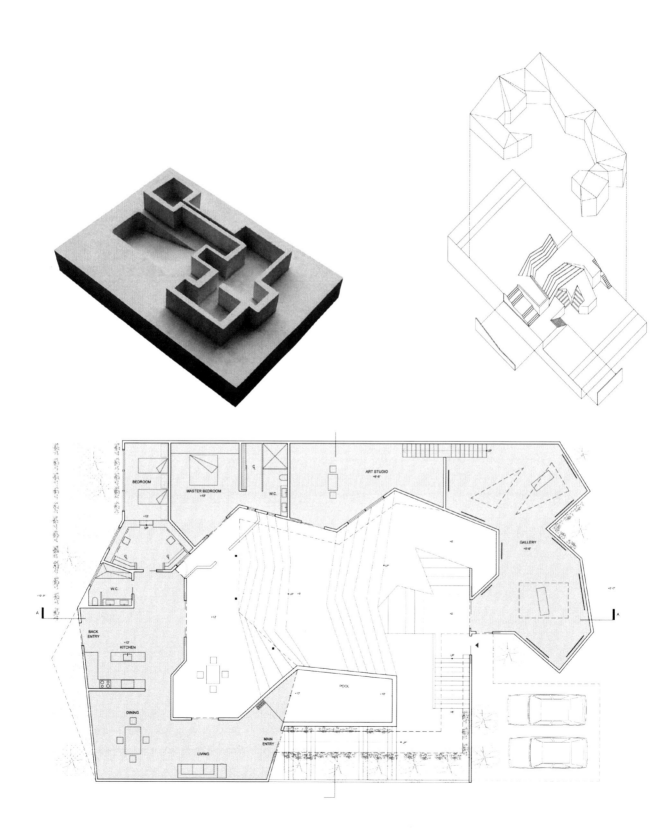

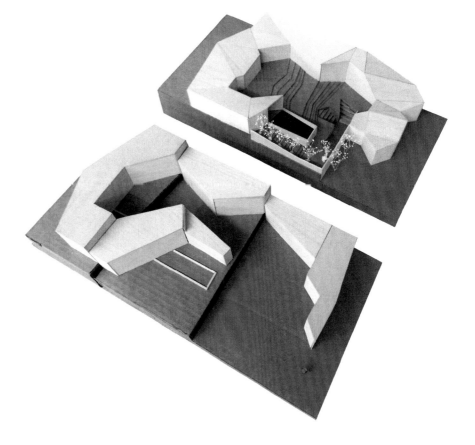

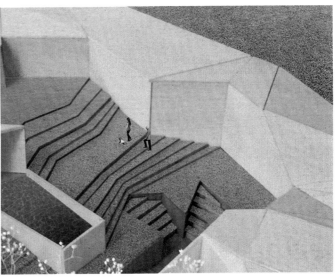

Kevan Kasmai
Melanie Perez

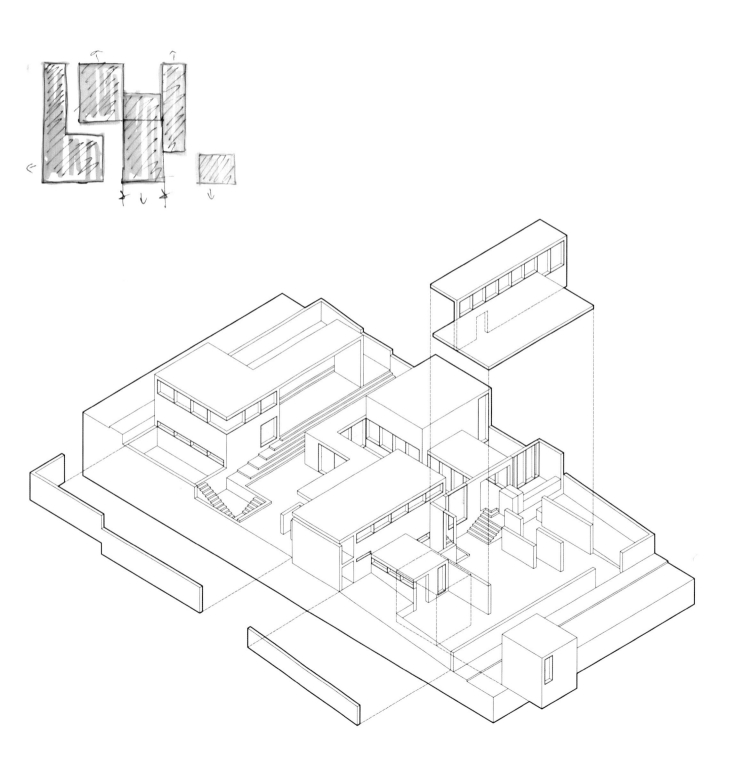

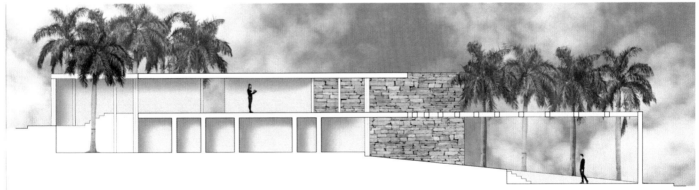

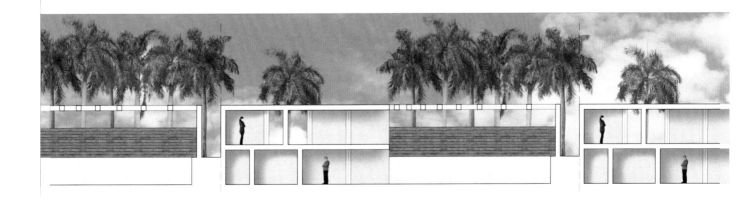

Design One

Nik Nedev *Coordi*
Jorge Balboa
Marco Campa
Sara Garaulet
Emmanuel Ferro
Elite Kedan
Arnaldo Sanchez

ator

Keven Kasmai
Emanuel Iral
Melanie Perez

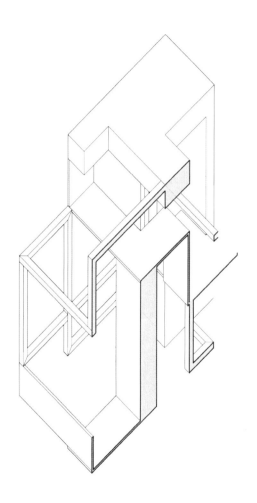

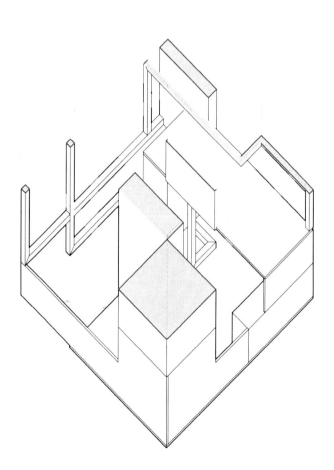

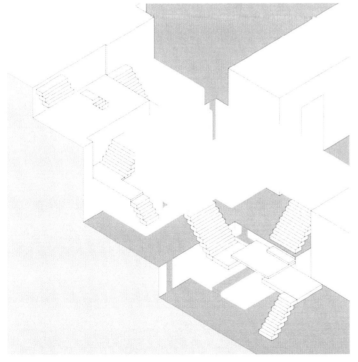
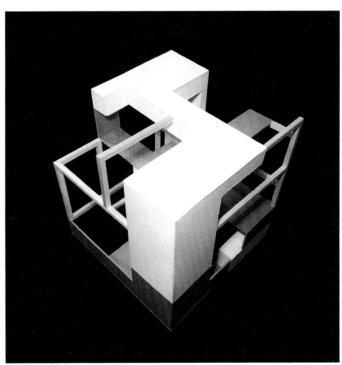

Yailyn Barrera
Briana Hunter
Stephanie Rico

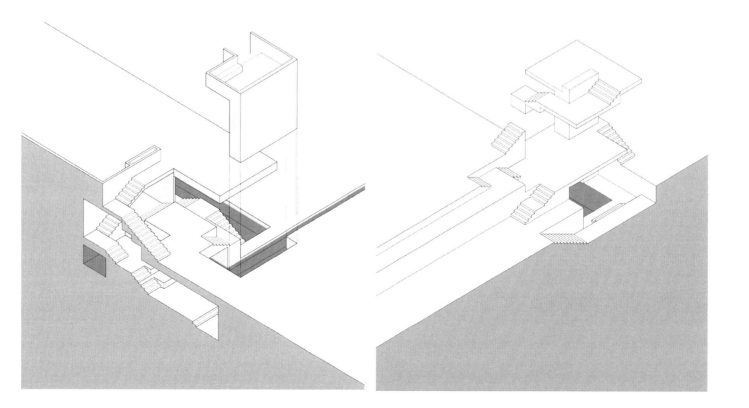

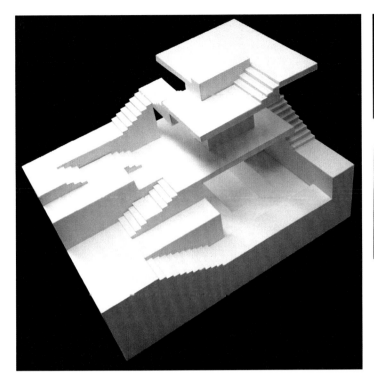

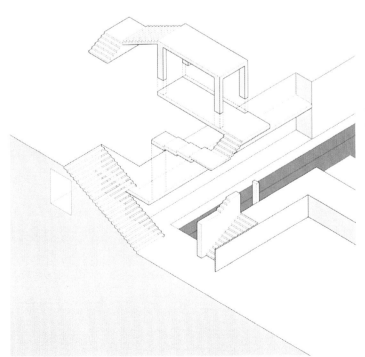
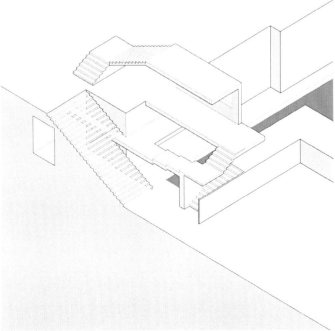

Miami
Matters
Four

Sand Spider
by Alastair Gordon

Folio
Alastair Gordon
Henry Rueda
Manuel Perez-Trujillo
Mrs. Elaine Walker

Images
Ezra Stoller
Alastair Gordon

We set out on our auspicious little outing to Sanibel, driving across the instep of Florida, marshy light deflecting off the windshield, Everglades sheet-flow expanding incrementally as we move westward along the pencil-straight line of Route 75, otherwise known as 'Alligator Alley', taking Route 41 and then Route 869 through Punta Rassa and across the sun-flecked causeway, now backed up with spring-break traffic all the way along Periwinkle Way and the far end of West Gulf Drive, where we finally turn into an unpaved driveway and find Paul Rudolph's little gem, the Walker Guest House, built in 1952.

The 24-by-24-foot frame rests on a bed of shells, high enough to catch breezes off the Gulf of Mexico and also withstand hurricane floods. An outrigger structure provides support for the ingenious, Rube Goldberg contraptions that Rudolph devised for raising and lowering eight large window flaps that are hinged along the top and operated with rope and pulleys.

Eight counterweight balls, made from cast concrete painted red, hang from cables and help to raise and lower the flaps, hence the nickname: "cannonball house".

Rudolph's vacation homes of this period signaled independence, self-sufficiency, and a lifestyle that was at one with the sun and sea. He worked with basic materials that could be found at any lumberyard and kept the price of construction and maintenance as low as possible. Standard lengths of two-by-four lumber were doubled up to create I-beam-style supports for the footings and the hurricane flaps were made from plywood and pegboard sandwiched together. The skeletal structure fulfilled Rudolph's desire to make the house "crouch like a spider in the sand", as he wrote, with spindly legs reaching out on all sides, eroding all sense of mass. The house's profile could change almost daily, depending on the weather, the season, the angle of light and the moods of the homeowners.

The sun is bright, almost blinding, as we walk up to the main house to meet Mrs. Elaine Walker, a spry 91 years old, warm and welcoming with a mischievous glint in her eyes.

"There was nothing here. It was the absolute boonies!" she says, laughing. "There wasn't even a telephone!" Wearing a blue-green dress and bone-white spectacles, she sits in a low-slung hammock chair, looking out at the liquid light rising off the Gulf of Mexico.

By the end of her first winter season on Sanibel, Elaine was learning to adapt to the quirkiness of Rudolph's little experiment in leisure living. "It was just like camping and I learned to be a good girl scout," she says, explaining how she grow to enjoy the most basic pleasures: swimming every morning, collecting shells, reading books. With only 580 square feet of internal living space, the house felt surprisingly expansive with its all-around views and basic geometry. The interior was divided into equal quadrants for dining, cooking, living and sleeping and couldn't have been simpler.

"You know, Mr. Rudolph told my husband that sometimes it's nice to be in a cave and sometimes it's nice to be in a pavilion," she said. "With the flaps down it was a cave. With the flaps up it was a pavilion."

With a few adjustments the flaps could also be made to funnel Gulf breezes through the house, as there was no air conditioning, but occasionally it was sweltering and Mrs. Walker remembers having to dive into the Gulf every half hour or so to keep cool. "I would never get out of my bathing suit."

The Walker Guest House received an inordinate amount of attention for such a modest commission. McCall's Magazineran a feature story in 1956 with a breezy text about the "house for carefree summer living." (Plans could be purchased from the magazine for 25 cents.) "I had no idea that our little guesthouse would become so famous," says Mrs. Walker. "It's really quite revered in the world of architecture."

Apart from a few minor repairs, the house is made of the same materials it was built with in 1952. Even the fixtures in the tiny kitchen and bathroom are original. Jack Priest, Mrs. Walker's son-in-law, stands in the doorway of the tiny guesthouse, wearing pink rubber clogs and a marlin-print shirt. He points to a metal escutcheon in the ceiling and explains how he has to replace one of the pull ropes every few years. "It takes real concentration," says Priest, who's learned how to guide the rope through the openings with a stiff wire.

While providing little more than shade and a place to sleep, the Walker Guest House expressed an open-ended lifestyle for a generation who'd survived World War II and were intent on building a brighter future. Today, the house can be seen as a ingenious prototype for sustainable living with its small footprint, self-cooling

cross breezes and simplicity of plan that was perfectly adapted for the subtropical climate of South Florida. Just as importantly, Rudolph's design was light-hearted, even whimsical in the midst of Cold War paranoia, with its dangling cannonballs and flip-top walls, fitting into the natural setting, and barely disrupting the sandy contours of the Sanibel beachfront. "I didn't come to appreciate the architecture for a long time," admits Mrs. Walker. "But it was wonderful to be living in a place that made my family so happy."

Taken from the Blog: Outdoor Cats in our MBUS website.

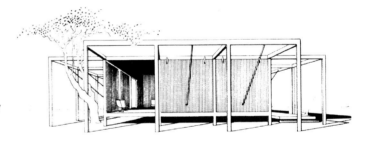

Facilities
Research / Essays
Bios

Fabrication Lab

Eric Peterson

10 am

Students are waiting outside for the Lab Assistant to open the door… three sheets of plywood, six bags of ready-mix concrete and two bags of plaster.

Students ask: "Is there a tool to cut concrete? How will I know when this concrete is ready to remove from the mold? What should I use to cut #4 rebar? What file type should I use for making something on the CNC machine? How much water should I add to this plaster mix?"

10:15 am

Students are milling one of the sheets of plywood on the CNC machine. The Lab Assistant is setting up files in RhinoCAM for the remaining pieces and evaluating 3d models for future projects.

Students ask: "What size bit is best for cutting acrylic? What type of glue is best for this material? How do I change the blade on this tool? Which sandpaper is best for this type of surface? What screw is best for attaching these materials together?"

11 am

Eight students arrive ready to continue working on the Bench Project. Two students set up at the 10" cabinet saw and begin milling recycled flooring. Several other students are outside the back door pulling nails and sorting materials for the milling team. Meanwhile, the rest of the team is using pneumatic nail guns, drills and screw guns to assemble the surface of the bench.

Students ask: "What is the difference between these nails? Is this glue good for exterior use?What is the difference between marine grade plywood and construction grade plywood? How much activator should I add to this resin? What can I use to cut a curve in this piece of wood?"

12:15 pm

The CNC Machine stops because of an error and everyone breathes a sigh – a few moments of quiet while we reboot and then start back up. A group of students arrive with some urban harvest of Cuban Mahogany for a table project.

Students ask: "Should we pre-cut the pieces before sending them through the 20" planer? What is the maximum size that fits in the drum sander? Which bandsaw is best for re-sawing wide materials? Why do I need to run these across the 6" joiner before ripping them on the table saw? How do you set up the biscuit joiner for thick materials?"

1:45 pm

Time to clean up Studio begins at 2. Clean up your area.

Students ask: "When can I get trained how to use the welder? I am going to the store – which polyurethane should I purchase? Can I make an appointment to review my model at 6 pm?

Who is the Lab Assistant tonight? Wait – can you cut this at 18"x32" for the Laser Cutter? I have a cutting appointment at 2 o'clock."

6 pm

Twelve students arrive to ask about building site models for a project in Caracas.

Students ask: "Should we use the CNC machine or the laser cutter? Which is the best software for topographic modeling? What kind of foam should we purchase for the topography? Which glue is best for polyiso foam? How do we join it to the base?"

7:30 pm

A student arrives to ask about electronics… they are embedding sensors and vibrating devices in a garment for an assignment in a seminar about mapping and perception.

Students ask: "What type of connector should I use to connect a battery? Is a crimp connector better than soldering the joints? Where can I buy heat shrink tubing? How do you measure resistance in a circuit? Can I borrow a soldering iron overnight?"

8:45 pm

Time to clean up! The lab closes at 9 pm. Clean up your area! But we are working on a faculty research project, we were told we could stay late and mill overnight – our faculty member will be here to supervise beginning at 9 p.m.

Students ask: "What are the safety procedures? Who do we call if there is a hardware problem? Which tools can we use and which are locked down?   Can we use the 12" compound miter saw? What are the cleaning and lock-up procedures when we are finished?"

10 pm

The CNC machine is humming along and students and faculty are busy working on research and prototype testing. The dust collector hums in the corner and the lights spill out onto the sidewalk. A pickup truck pulls up and a group of students unload logs they found by the side of the road - visions of a beautiful piece of furniture dance before their eye.

Digital Lab

Eric Goldemberg

The Digital Lab at the Department of Architecture operates as a support link between the studios, the seminar courses and the Fabrication Lab, enabling the visual speculation and representation of projects, and it serves as a practical laboratory extension of classroom theory. The Digital Lab integrates digital design and fabrication methodologies in architecture, with an emphasis on the versatility of tools and techniques offered to enhance the communication skills of the students. It contributes to establish a seamless workflow between 2D, 3D, and the different modalities of craft involved in the fabrication of architectural artifacts.

The output facilities of the Lab are organized to encourage the production of communication tools at many levels, including large format printing in 2D, scanning, laser-cutting and 3D printing. The Architecture Department hosts a very capable set of production facilities including both traditional analogue fabrication equipment and new rapid-prototyping fabrication and output tools to enable the production of architectural objects — both digital and physical - which reflect an open, critical engagement both with new and existing technologies. We encourage a collaborative environment when it comes to fabrication of model components; diversity of perspective is the foundation of innovative design.

The FIU SOA Digital Lab offers students and faculty in the Departments of Architecture, Interior Architecture, and Landscape Architecture the capacity to explore various modes of computer-aided reproduction and representation in both two- and three-dimensions.

The Digital Lab features a range of two-dimensional printers from simple sheet-fed Laserjets to wide-format roll-fed inkjet plotters, as well as a wide format scanner. Two laser cutters offer an opportunity to quickly produce surface studies or two-dimensional parts for models and assemblies. Several Makerbot replicators provide ample opportunity for rapid prototyping and formal exploration.

The practice of architecture relies on systems of communication to conceive, develop, and subsequently represent and communicate architectural ideas, where the breadth of the work is reflected in the implied proficiencies of technical skills and visual culture.

The Digital Lab takes a central role in the education of communications techniques and required skills sets offered across the architecture curriculum. It includes drawing tools ranging from generative diagramming to representation, project communication and project production documents. Students become familiar with established and emergent technologies and fabrication processes.

An understanding of iterative processes and transformation logics are critical in architectural design. As dynamical systems, transformational techniques allow technological practices to access the virtual. Transformational methods entail the manipulation of continuous surfaces or objects through procedures such as cutting, folding, and stretching. The precise manner in which an individual change will be redistributed over the whole cannot be predicted; each transformational procedure applies a pressure on the surface that generates other transformations across the surface. The interactions between these transformations comprise the 'versioning' power of the design techniques explored at the Digital Lab through different media.

The design environment at the Digital Lab contributes to the robust culture of making encouraged at the Department of Architecture, setting the foundation for understanding the implications of working within the framework of communication systems. It fosters excellence, precision and critical engagement, and encourages highly creative work in which working methods, tools and their interfaces are interlaced. The curriculum of the digital design classes responds to the constantly evolving paradigms of architectural communication, introducing new tools within a progressively structured program.

Set Lab

Shahin Vassigh

Co-Directors
Shahin Vassigh
Thomas Spiegelhalter

Every spring the PCA courtyard comes alive with the sound of breaking concrete. Each year students in Shahin Vassigh's concrete structures class design and build cast-in-place concrete beams to test for failure. All this activity happens in the courtyard of architecture department, just in front of new Structural and Environmental Technologies Lab/SET lab. Set behind an aluminum and glass curtain wall, this pristine white space is a workroom to build structural models, observe structural behavior and conduct hands on experiments. The lab construction was completed in summer of 2013 and it was furnished and ready to go in fall of 2013. In the short time it has been around, the lab has made a great impact on how students learn technology courses in our program. The main idea behind the design of the lab space are the type of equipment used and the design of each experiment, which is a collaboration and experiential learning that are proven to be effective in STEM education.

The room set up is extremely flexible with square tables that can accommodate group work. These tables are on wheels allowing the room to transform its configuration when needed. For example, in a truss bridge testing exercise, the tables are set in parallel rows allowing multiple bridges span through the gap between tables while being tested with load cells.Students in each participating course attend one lab per week. The lab sessions are organized around the lectures and are always associated with hands on investigations. Students conduct experiments with a range of hi-tech tools as well as low-tech devices that are designed and constructed by the teaching assistants. Currently, faculty and graduate assistants working at the lab are experimenting with using technology in a radically different way to improve learning. They have developed a prototype mixed reality model that combines Augmented Reality (AR) visualization with 3D digital printing. Augmented Reality visualizations- the ability to overlay computer information onto the real world in real-time is critical in developing the next generation of computer-based learning environments.

The designed prototype will allows students to interact with physical objects and learn about structural behavior that it would otherwise be impossible to observe. The SET-Lab is also used for the environmental design research with physical and digital diagnostic tools for individual or automated occupant thermal comfort controls. The occupant feedback is used to improve the lab operations associated with energy savings and CO_2e reduction. Students in the Environmental Systems courses use the collected data to run simulations on various software platforms that helps them to learn thermal comfort testing, monitoring, analysis, and validation.

Miami Beach Urban Studio

John Stuart

Thursday

2 pm

The history of Lincoln Road and the chain store go hand in hand. Lincoln, Cadillac, Saks Fifth Avenue, they've all been here. So why not start the afternoon with a delicious buttery chocolate croissant and a double iced Americano at Paul: French Bakery, (located at Paul: French Bakery, at) on 450 Lincoln Road in the splendid 420 Lincoln Building. But don't linger. Enjoy the sugar and caffeine rush during a pause on the monumental lobby stair to enjoy a view of the lovely Leo Birchansky murals from 1945 that express the integration of funding and education to create opportunity. Birchansky was a Russian artist and political cartoonist who fled to the United States when Stalin came to power and just seems to get what America is all about. Continue upstairs and join design reviews of students in the Architecture, Interior Architecture, and Landscape Architecture + Urban and Environmental Design departments. Take a break from helping the students and check out the exhibitions in the Design Gallery, the Main Gallery, the Long Hall Gallery, and the Fellows Gallery.

7 pm

After exhausting your lungs and mind with your comments on the students' exciting design work, refresh and reinvigorate your mind on the on the third floor of the 420 Lincoln building at the David Castillo Gallery, one of the hottest galleries in Miami and a leader in bringing the arts back to this end of Lincoln Road.

9 pm

Avoid the crush of the full-on weekend crowds and stroll west along Lincoln Road, stopping by to check out the latest model Tesla (a reference to the historic dominance of polo horses and then automobile showrooms on Lincoln Road) to the

Nespresso Boutique in the 1111 Lincoln Road building (Herzog + DeMeuron) for a quick pick-me-up espresso before heading up to the top floor in (1111 Lincoln Road the a) the purple elevator on Lenox Avenue to Juvia, the restaurant with arguably the most (specular) spectacular view in the city. Sit outside at the marble bar looking out over the restaurant and view with the lovely vertical tropical garden plants designed by botanist Patrick Blanc, known for such walls around the work from Spain to Japan. After a drink or two climb back down and find delicious sustenance at VISA-01 at 1680 Michigan for pizza and a salad. There are only six tables, so make a reservation and remember, it's a school night!

Friday
8 am
You're up early, energized by the amazing sunrise and cloudscape to hydrate, caffeinate, and head over to the newly renovated Flamingo Park Tennis Center, at 1200 Meridian Avenue. Start play at 7:30AM and finish up by 9AM. After you finish hitting, stay for a clinic for an extra dosage of cardiovascular workout. Be sure to notice the flocks of crows, parakeets, morning doves, and the (occasion) occasional Osprey or two who fly around in the drama that is continually transpiring overhead.

10 am
Pick up a Citibike and hike down to Joe's Stonecrab Take Away at 11 Washington Avenue for a bite of Stonecrab omelet. Keep your ears open. The business of Miami Beach will be taking place around you! After you've had your fill, both physically and politically, take a cruise through the Jewish Museum of Florida-FIU at 301 Washington Avenue. Look out for the special window donated by Miami Beach person of note, Meyer Lansky in the old synagogue that houses the museum.

2 pm
After learning about the Jewish History of Florida, indulge yourself in a new view of the history of modernity as told through objects and design by spending the rest of the day pouring over the many exhibitions and possibilities at The Wolfsonian-FIU, located at 1001 Washington Avenue. Lunch will be unnecessary. Fulfilment through art and intellectual pursuits will continue and can be augmented nicely by happy hour at the Betsy Hotel, one of the great literary hotels of the world. Look around at the exhibitions, talk to the writers in residences, read poetry and sip a delicious cocktail at the historic bar.

6 pm
If you have a hankering for chamber music, stop by the Urban Studios for a concert by the Amernet String Quartet, FIU's very own String Quartet in Residence. They are a remarkable group with enormous diversity of sound quality and repertoire. You may even be fortunate enough to hear a new work by the Miami Beach Urban Studios Composer in Residence and Martin Feldman acolyte, Professor Orlando Jacinto Garcia.

7:30 pm
Since you've already perused the Urban Studios, head quickly on out after the concert across the Miami Beach Soundscape Park designed by the Landscape Architecture firm, West 8. If there's a Wallcast that evening, by all means stop and enjoy. Otherwise, stop in at the lovely Regent Cocktail Club in the Gale Hotel at 1690 Collins for a refreshment before arriving at the Bass Museum of Art with the Arata Isosaki addition, located at 2100 Collins. It's open until 9PM on Fridays and the evenings are the best time to walk among the lovely sculpture garden that connects the museum to the beach. Spend time mulling over the mysterious figures cast

into the beach sand that covers the outside of the cylindrical auditorium building. This work from the 1960's is one of the most spectacular remaining works by Alberto Vrana, a sculptor known to experiment with new materials and mold-making processes. (a sculptor known to experiment with the experimental sculptor, Alberto Vrana).

9pm
Find your piece of tropical paradise and grab dinner at the Dutch Miami in the W Hotel South Beach at 2100 Collins Avenue. Make sure to leave room for the delicious salted lime pie for dessert. You'll need the extra calories for a walk up Collins Avenue for some late night music and chilling with the younger set at the Broken Shaker in the Freehand Miami at 2727 Indian Creek Drive.

Saturday
8 am
Wherever the night left you off, be sure to catch a sunrise on the beach and take a quick dip in the warm refreshing ocean. If the winds of fate carried you north near 71st Street and the historic Miami Modern Architecture, check out Rene Gonzalez's new North Shore Bandshell Park and Senior Center (at) on 501 72nd Street, while you sip an early morning cortadito prepared perfectly at Sazon Cuban Cuisine, located at 7305 Collins Ave. Or if fortune takes you back down south, jump into the Ocean on First Street, roll up and down the hills of South Pointe Park and fortify yourself at an outdoor table with a steak and eggs breakfast at Smith & Wollensky at 1 Washington Avenue, where you are invited to ponder the beautiful dance in the waves of fishing boats going out to sea and cruise ships returning to port - which (that) in some ways captures the fluidity and fragility that characterizes Miami Beach.

Faculty

Research / Essays

Jason Chandler
Infill Urbanism: Pedagogy, Policy and Building

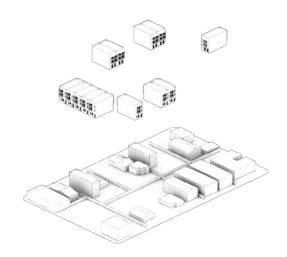

Infill Urbanism

Miami is a paradigm for two housing types: the single-family detached suburban house and the high-rise condominium. Both are vehicles of privacy, security and social separation. Miami is too young of a city to have enjoyed the infill urbanism of the 19th century. Except for some clusters in downtown Miami, Miami Beach, and Coral Gables, the city did not inherit a fabric of small-scale, mixed-use urban buildings. This "missing urbanism" constitutes an opportunity for Miami.

The infill building is a highly flexible urban proposal that both supports and treads lightly on existing urban contexts. As an act of coexistence, the infill building allows a given neighborhood the opportunity to grow without wiping out its valued older buildings or displacing its population for a more affluent one. The infill building confers value on the old and the new by occupying existing sites. By improving these sites, a neighborhood's history and culture are both preserved and enhanced for the future.

In contrast to suburban development, which does not completely occupy a buildable lot and requires expansion of services, infill urbanism utilizes the full potential of existing prepared sites. In an urban context, infilling supports the infrastructural investment of the city. Each urban site resides within services, networks and systems that enrich, support and protect its buildings.

The shape or limit of an existing urban site is both a dimensioned and legal configuration residing in the platted matrix of the overall city plan. When an infill project occupies an empty site, it incrementally contributes to the definition of the city plan. Over time, infill projects will help to define the pubic realm of the street with a fine grain of urbanism.

Pedagogy

Over last three years, in collaboration with Andrew Frey, a lawyer and developer, the Knight Foundation has supported the Design Six Infill Housing Studio with $80,000 of funding. This funding supported the travel of 17 faculty members and over 300 students to Savannah, three publications of the student work, and three public exhibitions (*Infill Variants* at Bas Fisher Invitational in 2013; *All Buildings Great & Small: New Building Designs for a Better City* at the Coral Gables Museum in 2014; and *Infill Housing: New Typologies* for Miami at the Barrio Workshop in 2015).

Pedagogically, the infill project requires students to reconcile a highly restricted urban site and embrace its potential repeatability. Tight site dimensions require students to solve spatial problems three-dimensionally and empirically account for all their design decisions. Repeatability requires students to develop street facades that reconcile the internal logic of their design with an understanding of the scale of the street.

The iterative process is both a means and end of this learning experience. Iteration is at the core of the architect's work and development. In a single project, the architect reworks, repeats and revises a scheme to perfect it. In the Infill Housing Studio, students confront recurring issues with a series of small projects and revisit precedence they encountered during their visit to Savannah. While it is based on reconciling the familiar, the iterative process allows for a critical platform for innovation to arise. Iteration embraces the notion of "testing" a design proposition. The initial idea may arise from a myriad of places, but once conceived, it can be applied to context and use and be developed to incorporate forces complementary and antithetical to its conception.

Policy
Parallel to the funded Infill Housing Studio was a successful effort to change the Zoning Code of the City of Miami. In an effort sponsored by Commissioner Francis Suarez and spearheaded by Andrew Frey, the Zoning Board and City Commission adopted a small building parking exemption. This new ordinance (14-01076 ZT1) exempted existing and new buildings, regardless of use, under 10,000 square feet in size from providing parking.

Previous to this progressive ordinance, parking requirements hindered the development of affordable housing in Miami. This insidious code requirement essentially institutionalized gentrification and the displacement of low-income communities. Simply stated, required parking increases the cost of housing. Developers are forced to absorb this expense and pass it on to the public. As a result, rents and housing prices are raised and the city can no longer support the diverse incomes of its populous.

This new ordinance will make housing more affordable in the City of Miami. Owners of small lots will be able to develop their properties more readily, empowering the local community to guide its own urban development. The increase of buildings without parking will also support investments in public transportation, walkability of neighborhoods, and the development of innovative ride-sharing systems.

Building
Over the past two years, my architectural practice has worked with Andrew Frey to design and build an affordable "townhouse" project. This project is in permitting and is slated for construction in 2016.

The townhouse is, for many American cities, an infill typology that creates dense, mixed-use neighborhoods. As a repeatable and small-scale intervention, it creates a fine grain of urbanism and clearly defined public space. For these cities, the townhouse has proven to be a durable building type that, after its inception as a single-family house, can be broken into smaller apartments or commercial uses. This adaptability transforms this 19th century building type into micro-apartment buildings for today's affordable housing needs.

Born from the townhouse, these micro-apartments are conceived as a prototype for the city. As compact infill urban buildings, these structures can be built incrementally over time on small or large lots. Small-scale development also expands participation in the growth of a city to its local constituents. With capital that is embedded in the local populous, the genius loci will engage the particulars of culture, construction, and neighborhood identity.

This proposal for two micro-apartments is located in the heart of Little Havana in the City of Miami. Each proposed structure is three stories tall and 4,500 square feet in size with (2) two bedrooms and (2) efficiency units. The front and back facades are open, and the sides are party walls. At 25'-0" wide, two buildings fit the typical Miami building lot. The building structure is composed of reinforced concrete block masonry with cast-in-place concrete slabs. As this project is an urban proposal, the development of façade was investigated. Each façade is composed of three bays, which are grouped and shifted to create a monumental asymmetrical frame of the city. This frame is conceived as green wall, a vertical garden for the street and an outdoor room for the residents.

Research / Essays

David Rifkind
Architectural responses to processes of modernization

I study architectural responses to processes of modernization, with special emphasis on the relationships between modern architecture and political forces. My first book, The Battle for Modernism: Quadrante and the Politicization of Architectural Discourse in Fascist Italy, examined modernism during Italy's twenty-year period of fascist rule. Based on my doctoral dissertation at Columbia University, the book focused on the circle of architects, artists, engineers, critics, theorists, and patrons who founded the influential journal Quadrante, whose polemical and militant promotion of modernism as the only appropriate cultural expression of fascist ideology provided an exceptional case study of the intersection between state interests and aesthetic concerns.

My subsequent research project, "Modern Ethiopia: Architecture, Urbanism and the Building of a Nation," is the first book-length study of the built environment in East Africa that incorporates field research in Ethiopia with archival research in Europe, the United States and Ethiopia. The project examines architecture and urbanism as evidence of the political and cultural transformations of Ethiopia during the first century of the country's modernization. The work approaches Ethiopia's modern history without presuming a decisive rupture between building techniques before and after the Italian invasion in 1935-36, and thus explores the possibility of hybrid construction methods and spatial configurations that synthesize native and foreign practices. "Modern Ethiopia: Architecture, Urbanism and the Building of a Nation" aims to fill several gaps in our understanding of African architecture and urbanism, Italian colonialism and the development of the many languages of modern architecture.

Architecture and urbanism in Ethiopia bear witness to the built environment's role in the production of national identities and engagement with processes of modernization and globalization. As the sole sub-Saharan nation to resist external dominance during the European "scramble for Africa," Ethiopia presents a rare opportunity to study the processes of modernization as directed by a non-Western country in the late nineteenth and early twentieth centuries. The growth of modern Ethiopia offers valuable insights into the relationships between political reforms, technological advancement, social transformation and the development of the built environment.

In the 1880s, Emperor Menelik II expanded the Abyssinian Empire to encompass nearly all of Ethiopia's current territory. Menelik immediately began an ambitious program of modernization in order to consolidate his power throughout the ethnically and religiously diverse nation. The emperor founded a new capital city – Addis Ababa – and established the institutions and infrastructures of a modern country, including a national currency and bank, an independent judiciary, a postal system, telephone and telegraph networks, municipal water and electricity services, and a railroad linking Addis to the Red Sea port of Djibouti. Menelik's successors, especially Haile Selassie I, expanded these efforts, and by 1930 Addis Ababa was a thriving metropolis whose diverse architecture reflected the city's cosmopolitan populace of Ethiopians, Armenians, Greeks, Indians, Yemenis, Sudanese and Arabs.

In both political and architectural terms, the Italian occupation of 1935-41 is often presented as a decisive break with Ethiopia's late imperial period, and popular histories often mistakenly attribute all the country's modern architecture to the Italians. Yet while Italian authorities commissioned and built a broad range of modernist structures, numerous continuities exist between colonial building practices and those of pre-invasion Ethiopia. The principal contributions of the Italians to the built environment of East Africa were through the introduction of new materials (such as concrete) and through urban design, which transformed settlement patterns radically and established the armatures for future metropolitan growth up to the present day.

This project studies the transformation of the built environment in Ethiopia between the founding of Addis Ababa in the 1880s and the present, in order to understand the country's responses to processes of modernization and globalization. How did the constructed realm respond to shifting relationships between public space and collective identity? What lessons do the architecture and urbanism of Ethiopia hold for the continuing development of appropriate local forms in a globalized world?

In addition to the historical scholarship, I have continued to practice architecture. In 2012, me and my wife, Holly Zickler, completed construction of our home in South Miami, which was designed to exceed the requirements for LEED Platinum and other benchmarking programs. We have shared our experiences with sustainable construction through tours, lectures and a blog, and have acted as consultants on sustainable construction for a local non-profit organization.

My current project, "Ideas for Miami," engages students and colleagues to develop suggestions for improving the sustainability of our city- either by technical means or by improving the quality of urban life. Ideas can be visionary or practical, for example, transforming elevated highways into linear parks with transit, or planting forests on the roofs of parking garages, or building beautiful bus shelters out of recycled glass. These ideas will be presented in drawings to the public, at first through a website and, as they develop, in a local exhibition and a publication. Together, these creative suggestions can offer a glimpse of what Miami might be like if it took the goals of sustainability seriously and supported the vibrant life of a dense city.

Research / Essays

**Marylis Nepomechie:
Collaborative | Trans-disciplinary |
Research | Pedagogy**

**MIAMI 2100: Envisioning a Resilient
Second Century
Marilys Nepomechie, FAIA
Marta Canaves, ASLA
Eric Peterson**

Our interdisciplinary Architecture | Landscape Architecture design studios on urban resilience represent some of the strategies and proposals produced through an NSF-funded multidisciplinary academic study of urban resilience in hot, humid, hurricane-prone coastal regions. Focused on the envisioned effects of sea level rise on the natural and built environments of urban coastal areas in Miami-Dade County, the larger work, of which the studios form one part and the Miami 2100 exhibition reflected more holistically, tracks the challenges and opportunities presented by a trans-disciplinary collaboration. Among the participants are scientists, engineers, water management districts, city and county government, cultural institutions, social scientists and of course designers. The work speculates on some of the opportunities afforded by climate change to critique, rethink, and transform our cities --and in that process ultimately to improve them. The studios and the exhibition that occupied over 50% of the exhibition space at the Coral Gables Museum for more than 30% of its annual calendar [November 2014 to March 2015] represented both a nascent pedagogy that seeks to take maximum advantage of transdisciplinary university research and engagement, and a nascent strategy for the data-driven study of resilience from the perspective of the design disciplines.

In 2010, Florida International University was awarded a grant from the National Science Foundation's ULTRA-Ex Program [Urban Long Term Research Area --Exploratory], in the division of Behavioral and Cognitive Sciences titled "Double Exposures: Socio-ecological Vulnerabilities in the Miami Dade Urban Region". That funding jumpstarted a broad range of trans-disciplinary academic explorations, for the first time involving the university's programs in architecture and landscape architecture. The result was a working team that has produced an array of academic work products since its inception, including a range of visioning studies. Part of a longer-term investigation that has since earned additional funding support from a number of external sources, the developing archive of projects created through this effort formed part of the MIAMI 2100 exhibition, and have been presented at a number of climate change seminars and symposia.

Extensively documented, long-term global warming trends are causing polar icecaps to melt, oceans to expand as their heat content increases, and sea levels to rise at accelerated rates Concurrently, aspects of climate change are altering weather patterns worldwide, changing the length of seasons, and increasing the intensity of seasonal storms, while causing both severe draughts and heavy flooding around the globe. In the hurricane-prone subtropics, and for urban areas built largely at or just above sea level, these conditions necessarily herald substantial, thoroughgoing physical change. Climate science holds that an increase in the atmospheric retention of greenhouse gases lies at the root of many of these conditions –and suggests that responsibility for these resides in human hands. While large-scale, sustained, deliberate and targeted preventive action may slow some of the predicted change, the desired results are not guaranteed, and the need for planned resilience is unequivocal. In South Florida, conservative estimates predict a rise in sea levels between one and two meters over the next century. With it will come extensive flooding, as well as challenges to all the infrastructures that enable daily life.

According to the UN Atlas of the Oceans, over 44% of the world's population currently lives within 150 kilometers of a coast, most of these sites at low elevations. With the rapid increase in urban coastal populations and tourism, the magnitude of the trials ahead are difficult to overestimate. Significant repercussions for life safety, food security and public health, as well as for urban infrastructure, connectivity, and every sector of public and private life are among the myriad quandaries posed by climate change. Around the globe, difficulties will vary in intensity and urgency. As a result of many variables, including elevation, geological composition, subtropical location, hydrological systems, availability of fresh water, and level of urbanization, the challenges for South Florida, are acute.

Sea level rise poses problems with implications for the form and infrastructure of our cities and for the development of new ways to imagine their built fabric. New building typologies, environmental, structural and building construction systems, as well as new building materials and processes for building assembly will all be required elements of our urban resilience. At FIU, we have begun to address some of the many changes that lie ahead, viewing them as previously untapped opportunities to improve aspects of our city, even as we seek ways to heighten its longterm resilience.

Work completed through our design studios has incorporated input from --and participation in—a series of public design charrettes organized by the Southeast Florida Climate Compact in conjunction with the Consulate of the Netherlands in Miami. These 'Dutch Dialogues' have brought together expert climate consultants,

policy and governmental agencies, community groups, design and engineering professionals, as well as academics. The charrettes and studios have produced a number of possible avenues for investigation. Among them are proposals for improved, raised, and multi-modal public transportation systems, improved, networked communications infrastructure, new elevated buildings and public spaces, new and retrofitted structures that are increasingly energy independent and reliant on renewable resources, all forming part of an urban structure that responds to –and thrives on-- increased levels of water in our environment.

By means of drawings, models, digital visualization, and narrative texts, our research and pedagogy expand discussion about the range of possible responses to our environmental vulnerabilities, and about the role of the academy in facilitating and informing that process. Simultaneously, they reveal unexpected opportunities to improve an extraordinary urban place even as it builds resilience across a range of fronts.

Research / Essays

Gray Read: What role do buildings play in the the theater of urban life?

What role do buildings play in the theater of urban life? And what design strategies of urbanism can architects learn from the past? My research centers on reconstructing the architectural tradition of design for social life in cities, a tradition grounded in urban experience and apparent in building design, yet rarely articulated in words. This knowledge of how to design places to support the vital life of the city is particularly needed now in response to a demand for urban convenience and sustainability, as young people who grew up in American suburbs are now moving into town seeking a vital cultural and professional life. And the nation must achieve sustainability. Vibrant, dense cities offer the most broadly accessible response to climate change. Studies show that people who live in dense cities use a fraction of the energy of their suburban counterparts without expensive technology or extraordinary effort, simply because of the inherent efficiencies of proximity. Cities can offer a good life to people at all income levels at minimal carbon cost. The challenge for architects is to design buildings not just in the city, but of the city, which contributes to the quality of urban life- socially, technically, and aesthetically. To meet that task, my research looks back to the vibrant life of cities and through analyzing buildings and texts, I propose explicit architectural strategies that support the social fabric.

Two books and an edited volume focuses on different aspects of the question. Most recently, Modern Architecture in Theatre: the experiments of Art et Action (Palgrave Press, 2014) focuses on the close allegiance between the art of urbanism and that of theater in the moment of nascent modernism in early 20th century Europe. The book reconstructs the work of Edouard Autant, a Parisian architect active in the 1920s, who developed a theory of social space through experiments in theater. Autant, Louise Lara, and their acting troupe Art et Action presented performances with innovative set designs gave actors spatial contrasts (high/low, near/far) to develop dramatic relationships. Autant designed performance spaces that set up specific relationships between those who watch and those who are watched, which mirror and comment upon the characteristic spaces and events of urban life. Autant and Lara's work can be read as a treatise on the nature of performance inherent in all aspects of social life.

Architecture as a Performing Art (Ashgate Press, 2013), edited with Marcia Feuerstein, presents essays written by architectural historians and practitioners that explore the intersection between theater and architecture, reaching deep into history as well as examining current practices. Scholars reveal a profound metaphoric link between design and social order, first in the origins of theater itself, then in mythic plays performed in the amphitheaters of ancient Greece. The idea that the city and its buildings were the theater of social life explicitly informed architectural practice in the classical tradition, and was continually reinvented into the 20th century. Recently, architects have again embraced theater as an inspiration in the design of spaces that present people well.

The Miniature and the Gigantic: Essays on Human Scale in Philadelphia Architecture (Mellen Press, 2007) examines the vernacular architecture of the city of Philadelphia to discover how the buildings gave dimension to urban life, both physically and poetically. Life on the ground was measured in classical architecture that gave proportion to all elements in relation to each other and to the human body, from the layout of the city as a whole, which oriented citizens in the landscape, to the details of the steps, bricks and windows. Above the cornice line of the traditional city, a miniature architecture of cupolas and steeples met the sky, while below the ground, infrastructure made the metaphoric arteries and gastric system of a giant urban body. The art of scale was central to classical architectural education and to the practices of construction that built the city.

The ideas explored in research inform my classes in Architectural Theory and studio, which develop both analytical and design skills. Theory classes ask, "how do buildings act socially with and among people," and "how do they act environmentally within the local ecosystem." Students analyze buildings in drawings and explain their discoveries in writing. In studio design classes, my students often focus on Miami, analyzing the city and creating projects to support both the social and natural life of the city we know well. In one studio, students created and performed short skits that included an architectural actor that they had designed and built.

My current project, "Ideas for Miami," engages students and colleagues to develop suggestions for improving the sustainability of our city- either by technical means or by improving the quality of urban life. Ideas can be visionary or practical, for example, transforming elevated highways into linear parks with transit, or planting forests on the roofs of parking garages, or building beautiful bus shelters out of recycled glass. These ideas will be presented in drawings to the public, at first through a website and, as they

develop, in a local exhibition and a publication. Together, these creative suggestions can offer a glimpse of what Miami might be like if it took the goals of sustainability seriously and supported the vibrant life of a dense city.

Research / Essays

Shahin Vassigh and Winifred Newman: Mixed Reality and Collaborative Learning

Project team: Shahin Vassigh and Winifred Newman, Architecture Shu-Ching Chen and Scott Graham, Computer Science

The aim of the project is described to develop a teaching tool for facilitating collaborative and experiential learning. Recent research shows combining physical models with overlay of digital information and visualization techniques can enhance learning. The hypothesis is that cognitive learning is enhanced when students are able to manipulate and jointly construct a physical object while sharing knowledge about that object in a "mixed reality" environment. The main thrust for developing this tool is to alter the traditional use of physical architectural models as a representational instrument. Architectural models are often used to communicate ideas about tectonics, massing and general organization of buildings. Students spent significant amount of time and effort to make and refine these models, however a deeper learning is undermined by focusing on the formal aspect of the model rather than the performative aspects of the actual building.

Utilizing Augmented Reality (AR) technology for embedding critical lessons and information with respect to materiality, performance metrics, systems capabilities and the carbon footprint of building elements into architectural models transform them into "smart objects". Using smart object to construct or assemble building models in a collaborative process can be an effective way to enhance learning, particularly in the area of sustainable design and construction that is driven by the performative aspects of buildings.

To achieve this, the project team is developing "ecoblox"- a learning tool that consists of three components: 1) a kit of parts comprised of small-scale physical models of building elements with embedded AR markers, 2) the ecoBlox application, and 3) a number of scenarios with detailed instruction and program for building design. The kit of parts are 3D printed small-scale elements with a number of variations and extensive choices representing building elements such as floor plates, walls, roofs, structure and mechanical systems. Each element has an embedded AR code that is activated with the camera of a cell phone, or another handheld device. The ecoBlox application includes a digital catalogue of each building element with physical properties and attributes such as specific weight, size, thermal resistance (R-Value), rate of heat loss (U-Factor), embodied energy, embodied water, and the initial and cost.

As students work together and use physical model elements to assemble a building in response to a design scenario, they learn about the attributes of each component by activating the AR code and receiving information through audio narrated text, 3D visuals, virtual case studies, simulations, interactive drawings and tabulated metrics. This technology allows students to receive information on-demand for the task at hand. In addition, it helps students to learn from each other through negotiation, evaluation of alternatives and selection of building elements. The eventual goal is to enhance students' ability to design with building performance as a significant goal. This tool is primarily designed to enhance the sustainable design education. However, it could be used in technology courses and laboratories or integrated into design studios.   The integration of ecoBlox in design studios could be in terms of a series of studio exercises that prepares students to engage in their own design proposals. By using the ecoBlox prior to their design project, students will become aware of how their design choices impact the sustainability of their building.

Bio

Jason R. Chandler, A.I.A
Chair and Associate Professor in the
Department of Architecture
Jason completed a Master of Architecture
from the Graduate School of Design at
Harvard University and a Bachelor of
Architecture from Cornell University. He
is Principal of Chandler and Associates,
Architecture

Alfredo Andía
Associate Professor
Alfredo completed a Ph.D. at U.C. Berkeley,
a Master's Degree from Harvard University,
and an Architectural degree from Universidad
Catolica of Valparaiso. His work combines his
interest and expertise in architectural design,
advanced technologies and the future of
practice. He recently co-authored the book
"Post-Parametric Automation in Design
and Construction."

Malik Benjamin
Instructor
Malik completed a Master of Architecture
– Computing & Design and Urban Desing
from the University of Miami and a Bachelor
of Architecture from Cornell University. He
is the founder of CreativeMornings/Miami
and Awesome Foundation. He serves on
the Young Patrons Executive Committee

of the Patricia and Phillip Frost Museum of
Science, Miami Dade County Art in Public
Place Selection Committee and Architecture
& Engineering Services Selection Committee.

Claudia Busch
Instructor
Claudia completed a Diploma Certifi
cate in Architecture from the F.H. Hamburg,
Germany and an MS in Advanced
Architectural Design from Columbia
University. She is a principal in the firm BBA /
Berenblum Busch Architecture.

Jaime Canaves
Professor, FAIA
Jaime completed a Master and a Bachelor
of Architecture at the University of Florida.
He is the founder of the FIU Department of
Architecture Walk on Water Competition,
which celebrated its 25th year in 2014.

Adam Drisin
Associate Professor
Adam completed a Master of Design
Studies from Harvard University and holds
a professional degree in Architecture from
Cornell University. He is the founding Co-
Director of the design discipline for the
National YoungArts Foundation and serves
as Co-Chair of the Selection Committee to
nominate Presidential Scholars in Design for
the US Commission on Presidential Scholars.

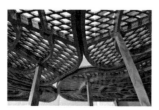

Nick Gelpi
Assistant Professor
Nick completed a Master of Science in
Advanced Architecture Design at Columbia
University and a Bachelor of Architecture
from Tulane University. His recent work

includes the winning proposal for the
Wynwood Gateway Park competition, an
international design competition for which
he and fellow FIU Professor Roberto Rovira
received first place.

Eric Goldemberg
Associate Professor
Eric completed a Master of Science in
Advanced Architectural Design at Columbia
University. Eric serves as Digital Design
Coordinator and teaches graduate studios
and advanced digital design and fabrication
courses. He co-founded MONAD Studio with
Veronica Zalcberg.

Mark Marine
Professor and Visiting Instructor, Fall 2014
Mark completed at Master of Architecture
at the University of California at Los Angeles
and a Bachelor of Science in Architectural
Studies at Florida International University.
Mark is co-founder and principal of Danger
Marine Design.

Nikolay Nedev
Instructor
Nikolay completed a Master of Architecture
in Urban Design at the Harvard Graduate
School of Design and a Bachelor of
Architecture at the University of Miami. He
serves as the Pre-Graduate Coordinator.
His academic interests include Typology
and Design Methodology in the work of
Le Corbusier, as well as, the relationship
between Art and Architecture.

Marilys Nepomechie, F.A.I.A
Professor and IDP Educator Coordinator
Marilys completed a Master of Architecture
from the Massachusetts Institute of
Technology, a Bachelor of Arts, English
Literature from the University of Florida and
has been inducted to the AIA College of
Fellows. Her writing, research, urban design
and building projects focus on the cultural,
social and environmental contexts of design.

Winifred E Newman
Associate Professor, Director
of Advanced Studies
Winifred completed a Ph.D., M. Phil and M. Arch from Harvard University and a B. Arch and B.S. from University of Texas at Austin. Her research focuses on neuroscience and architecture.

Eric Peterson
Instructor and Fabrication Lab Manager
Eric completed a Master of Architecture from the University of Florida and a Bachelor of Arts degree from Middlebury College. An accomplished carpenter, Eric served his joinery apprenticeship under Master Builder Charles Farrell. His academic expertise is introductory design studio pedagogy; his research focuses on fabrication, prototyping and furniture design.

Gray Read
Associate Professor
Gray completed a PhD from University of Pennsylvania. Her most recent publication, Modern Architecture in Theater: The Experiments of Art et Action (Palgrave, 2013), focuses on how the art of theater informs architectural design. Her current project, in collaboration with FIU students, is to develop design ideas to enhance urban life in Miami.

David Rifkind
Associate Professor
David completed a PhD at Columbia University, a Master of Architecture at McGill University and Bachelor of Architecture at the Boston Architectural Center. He teaches courses in architectural history, theory and design. His research deals with the relationships between politics, culture and the built environment since the late nineteenth century, with special emphasis on Italy and Ethiopia.

Camilo Rosales, .A.I.A
Associate Professor
Camilo completed a Master of Architecture II at Harvard University, and a Master of Architecture and Bachelor's with Honors from the University of Texas at Austin. His work focuses on human- environment transactions; this has been mostly expressed through built works in the U.S and Central America and by writings and grant projects.

Henry Rueda
Visiting Instructor Spring 2015
Henry completed a Diploma de Arquitecto from the Facultad de Arquitectura y Urbanismo at Universidad Central de Venezuela and a Master of Sciences in Advanced Architectural Design from Columbia University. His work focuses on single family houses in Latin America.

Thomas Spiegelhalter
Associate Professor
Co-Director of the Structural and Environmental Technologies Laboratory
Thomas has realized in Europe and the US, numerous solar zero-fossil-energy building realizations projects and large-scale sustainability master planning. As a result of his 25 years of design/built work, research, teaching, He has received 53 prizes, awards and honors in competitions, individual and in collaboration with landscape architects and engineers.

John Stuart
Professor and Associate Dean for Cultural and Community Engagement, Executive Director of the Miami Beach Urban Studios
John completed a graduate degree in Classical Archaeology from Princeton University, a Master of Architecture from Columbia University and undergraduate degrees in Classics and Applied Mathematics from Brown University.

Shahin Vassigh
Professor and Co-Director of the Structural and Environmental Technologies Laboratory
Shahin completed a Master of Architecture, a Master of Urban Planning and a Bachelor of Science in Civil Engineering from the University at Buffalo, the State University of New York.

Her work has been characterized as setting new standards for new media educational materials and is published and distributed internationally.

Study Abroad
Genoa

While study abroad in Italy for architecture students has its traditional attractions and justifications, the FIU program in Genoa aims at a different type of experience, one that is critical and reflective and takes advantage of its unexpected context. Genoa has a variety of urban fabric and spatial types, and architectural works ranging from the medieval through the nineteenth century, to significant interwar and post war Modern works of architecture, and finally to contemporary architectural works that are part of Genoa's ongoing project of renovation to establish its identity in the 21st century. While in Genoa, students are guided to develop an understanding of contemporary and modern architectural design grounded in disciplinary knowledge and changing social and cultural contexts.

Alexis Ortega described her experience studying abroad in Genoa: "Making Genoa my home for this past semester was truly a life changing experience, both personally and professionally. Its authenticity inspired me and allowed me to find out a little more of who I am and what I want. Through our many trips in Europe, I have acquired a new vision of architecture, and I believe this has made me a better and more conscious designer. My experience was everything and more than what I had hoped for."

Claudia Lopez / Maria Franco
Victoria Rein / Daniel Butto

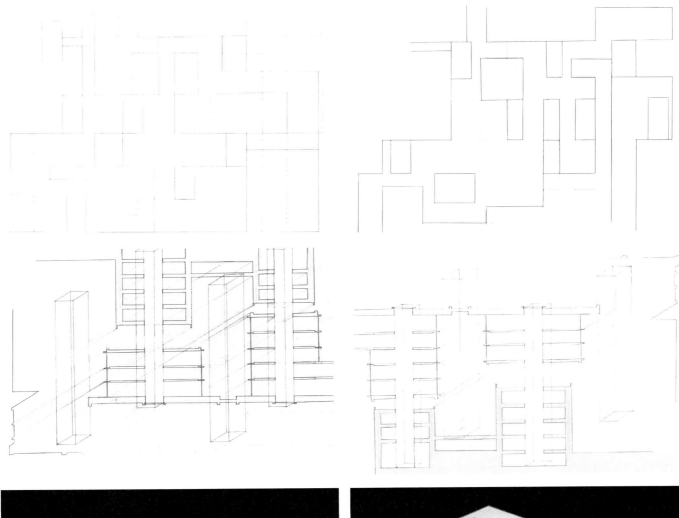

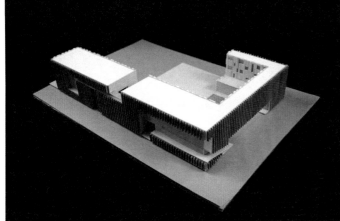
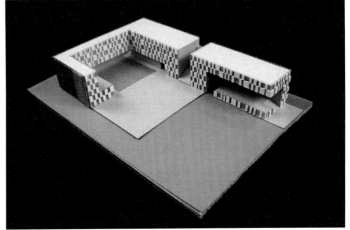

Study Abroad
London / Berlin

From May 10th to 24th, 2014, FIU architecture students studied abroad in London and Berlin, under the guidance of Professor Marilys Nepomechie, Professor Jaime Canavés, Instructor and Fabrication Lab Manager Eric Peterson, and Instructor and Lower Division Coordinator Claudia Busch.

The capital cities of Germany and the United Kingdom served as classroom and base for their studies, allowing students to gain first-hand experience of urban centers rich in history and (re)invention. In each city students visited historical and contemporary projects - structures and spaces that have set new international standards for design and engineering practice. The visits supported research and critical thinking on the subjects of urban resilience and sustainability.

Studio and elective offerings engaged students through case studies; through the art and technology of film and videography; through emerging models of graphic analysis and visualization; and through the design of urban infrastructure and public space. In Miami, students designed two pedestrian bridges - one crossing the Thames River in London, and the other crossing the River Spree in Berlin. Through the two accompanying seminars, students created videos and maps to document, analyze, and interpret their experiences abroad.

Among the sites visited in London were the Serpentine Gallery in Kensington Gardens; Royal Institute of British Architects Gallery; the Architectural Association; the John Soane and British Museums; Roman wall and amphitheater; the Tower of London and London City Hall; the Tower Bridge and Museum; Lloyds of London; St. Paul's Cathedral; the Millennium Bridge and Herzog de Meuron's Tate Modern; the offices of Zaha Hadid Architects and RTKL; Olympic Park; Thames Barrier the O2, and Canary Wharf. While in Berlin, students visited the Berlin Dom, Mies van der Rohe's New National Gallery, Scharoun's Philharmonic Concert Hall; Liebeskind's Jewish Museum, Peter Eisenman's Holocaust Memorial; Zumthor's Topography of Terror; Gehry's DZ Bank; Nouvel's Gallerie Lafayette; Foster's Reichstag; the Altes and Pergamon Museums; Potdsdamer Platz, the IBA residential projects, and the Gropius Bauhaus Archives..

Study Abroad
London / Berlin
Marilys Nepomechic
Jaime Canaves
Eric Peterson
Claudia Busch

London

Study Abroad
London / Berlin
Marilys Nepomechie
Jaime Canaves
Eric Peterson
Claudia Busch

Marilys Nepomechie
Jaime Canaves
Eric Peterson
Claudia Busch

Berlin

Study Abroad
London / Berlin
Marilys Nepomechie
Jaime Canaves
Eric Peterson
Claudia Busch

Study
Abroad
Paris /
Milan

Paris to Milan: Five Points to Skycraper Urbanism

From May 12th to 25th, 2014, students traveled to Paris and Milan. David Rifkind (Professor), Malik Benjamin (Instructor and Director of Program Innovation), Nik Nedev (Instructor), and Shahin Vassigh (Professor) guided and taught the group of students.

The theme of this study abroad excursion was "Paris to Milan: Five Points to Skycraper Urbanism."

Students studied in the cities of Paris, Besancon, and Lyon in France and Milan in Italy. While in France, they visited the Louvre, the Bibliothèque Sainte-Geneviève, the Panthéon, the Arab World Institute, and Center Pompidou. They also visited structures like Maisons Jaoul, La Roche, Villa Planeix, Ronchamp, and La Tourette. In Milan, they toured the Duomo, Galleria Vittorio Emanuele II, the Castello Sforzeco, and Casa Rustici. Towards the end of their trip, students took a day trip to Lake Como by train to explore the villas along the lake.

Study Abroad
Paris / Milan
Malik Benjamin
David Rifkind
Shahin Vassigh
Nikolay Nedev

Milan

Study Abroad
Paris / Milan
Malik Benjamin
David Rifkind
Shahin Vassigh
Nikolay Nedev

Malik Benjamin
David Rifkind
Shahin Vassigh
Nikolay Nedev

Paris

Study Abroad
Paris / Milan
Malik Benjamin
David Rifkind
Shahin Vassigh
Nikolay Nedev

Study
Abroad
Tokyo

Japan: A Look into Contemporary Japanese Architecture and Environment Sustainaiblity Strategies for Tokyo

Students studied abroad in Japan with Associate Professor Alfredo Andia, Associate Professor Camilo Rosales, Associate Professor Eric Goldemberg, and Associate Professor Thomas Spegielhalter from May 12th to May 24th, 2014.

The study abroad program focused on visits to many examples of contemporary Japanese architecture, Japanese design, and environment sustainability strategies for the city of Tokyo.

During the program, students visited the Edo-Tokyo Museum, the Omotesando District, Odaiba Artificial Island, Shibuya, Ahoyama neighborhood, the National Art Center, and the Yokohama Pier. On their itinerary was also the Tokyo International Forum, the Senso-Ji Temple, the Imperial Palace East Gardens, Ueno Park, the Tokyo National Museum, and the Gallery of Horyuji Treasures. Additionally, students visited the firms of Takeshi Hosaka and O+H Architects.

The Japan Architecture Program will focus on the contemporary architecture, urbanism, and urban culture in Japan. The program will begin with a two week trip to Tokyo, Kyoto, and Teshima Island in which we will visit a large number of extraordinary examples of contemporary and traditional architecture and practices. In the studio, and the 2 electives, we will observe how contemporary Japanese architecture is increasingly more interested in bare experiences that reveal the state of the "now" in our life.

Study Abroad
Tokyo
Alfredo Andia
Eric Goldemberg
Camilo Rosales
Thomas Spiegelhalter

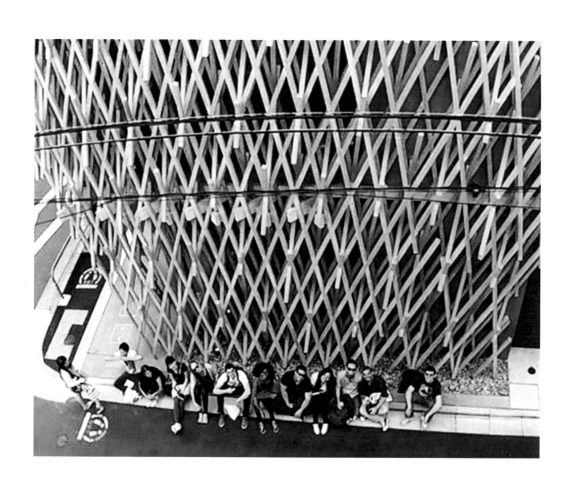

Study Abroad
Tokyo
Alfredo Andia
Eric Goldemberg
Camilo Rosales
Thomas Spiegelhalter

Miami
Matters
Five

Miami 2100

Transcripts from video interviews

Folio
Alistar Gordon
Roberto Rovira

Images
Branko Mimic

Excerpt from an interview
with Alistar Gordon

My name is Alistar Gordon, and I'm a cultural historian and a critical journalist and I'm very interested in the problem of how a place like Miami rebrand itself as an aware international city of 21st century and to do that it's gonna be a lot of not just engineering and legal work and political work but reimagining what a city like this could be because it's based on this resort history which is very of the surface of the moment is like a poster in other travel's perfect beach of perfect water the perfect sky and no one wants to go to mess with that because that's has been the money generator for all these generations so I feel like the best thing I can do as a writer and as a cultural historian is to help people start to understand how you can actually create what I call a trope, a positive metaphor or trope for not just dealing with issues that are coming up environmental issues but actually the even taking the lead the other with the Netherlands is now excepted that they're going to be underwater in the most of the Netherlands reclaimed from the north sea now their motto is invite the ocean in and that I think it away Miami has to at one side invite the ocean invite Atlantic Ocean in the other side invite Everglades to invite the Everglades again because the cities is caught between these two bodies of water through problematic and I don't think theres another city in the world like that so in a sense it's I think one needs to begin creating very positive imaginative and innovative solutions that may not ever get build but starts a dialogue so the newspapers are running it the television is running it museums are discussing like this show it and eventually you you might be able talk you into something that quite not only convincing but actually workable in the future, you know one of the things that I have been working on recently is in the way of creating a narrative for how you find out about rediscovering or rebranding a city like Miami and one of the things you can do is sort of look for often in history you bypass some of the best metaphors in the best narratives that can be reused recycle for the future and I always think of this line of that somehow the future is always embedded in the past realize as a cultural historian and a writer you have to go back and look and find these traces and is very hard because is very superficial you know it's swimming pools and hotels and this sort of land booms and schemes kind of crazy and people make a lot of money very short amount of time and then the loose it very quickly but the cycles are much faster than in the rest of the country and I think that's what the developers and some in the city government kind of depend on this five to ten year profit cycle which is of course insane for example the dutch have a five year, ten year even a hundred year plan for virtually almost everything they do, so until Miami gets in that kind of head nothing's is really going to change but I do think there's this wonderfully rich legacy of architecture landscape and water that has been the cities have been built on and no one have taken a look at that seriously, now they have these water shows that they would happen in 1930s and 40s, One of the reasons Florida have spring water that was incredibly clear to photograph under water they would do Hollywood movies underwater here and this early notion that a lot of the first the first military became down here during summer wars they spoke about the water as if like the sky here so this is a combination of translucency and at an transparency with this sky and the water I think is a beautiful notion, maybe you can even build a whole city based on that rebuild the city you have canals running east to west from the ocean flooding into the Everglades like nature used to do and we replenished the Everglades and vice versa you know there are all kinds of it is like that I think on the student level on a creative level on artistic level even on a novelistic writing level you can you can start imagine the possibilities and you have to do that before the real thing happens and I don't think we're any down here in South Florida anywhere close to that realization of what you might be able to do because the old paradigms of your short profit cycle the resort cycle like don't buy me out by telling me about pollution or in a rising sea levels that has to be replaced by something much more in the in the real world of the 20 century.

Excerpt from an interview
with Roberto Rovira

My name is Roberto Rovira I'm the chair of landscape architecture environmental and urban design at Fiu, to the question of sea level rise and urban resilience, I think that the topic of resilience is absolutely essential in how we think of ourselves and how we envision a future here in Miami in particular, however I think that it's equally important that we change that question around a little bit cannot just consider our answers to be about resilience but rather how we can make our cities thrive our particular region thrive to me it's about driving style just about surviving or just being resilient and that means that we really have to think holistically we have to think about not just the solutions the physical solutions that address the issue that are before us the threats there before us the rather how we build a society how we go to city that is completely comprehensive in the way to understand that relationship that means involving the arts that means involving design involving architecture landscape architecture interior architecture all of these different fields should ultimately work together to understand the condition that does not just affect us physically but really it it's it impacts the way that we live and in order to live in Orchard Drive we have to understand ourselves as being far more than just a product of our physical environment in terms of how we can engage the public in the process of thinking about him bar mitzvah designing the environment I really has to do with an exposure of ideas the more that things are hidden the more that we don't make an effort to bring these things to the surface by allowing people to see how buildings function allowing people to see what the relationship of land and water is allowing people to understand how they build and how that is connected to the environment less we make those relationships explicit middle be a lot harder for people to understand the context and the conditions that affect them so I feel that it's really a responsibility of a designers to create an DesignWorks that allowed us to expose these these relationships rather than create buildings are completely hermetically sealed from the environment we should really make an effort to design cities and buildings and architecture and landscape centrally work together so that you can fully understand that where you are where you live has everything to do with with the place and isn't completely independent of that you should know that south Florida depends on its relationship to water and has probably since the very beginning this is been essential to why the cities here and Whitecity is going so we should embrace that designers and part of that is educating the public about these things in the way that we build in the way that we design in terms of possibilities and alternatives to design I think we have every reason to think big to think long-term to think about the big gesture that will presumably solve all the problems related to sealevel rise, is our responsibility to do that however we also have to understand that any change in any city in any society it's about increments, and increments have this short lifespan that is more immediate and allows us to relate to our environment a lot more closely so I think that it's as much a need to think long-term think of the big master solution as it is essential for us to think short term to think what kinds of solutions now within five years within 10 years with in two years what has the solutions now are appropriate are consistent with a long-term vision even if we cannot bring to bear all of our resources that wants to create that wonderful solution that might be more visionary so we need to think in a visionary way but we also need to act in a very pragmatic way I think that's a perfect challenge for design.

Lectures /
Events

Lectures

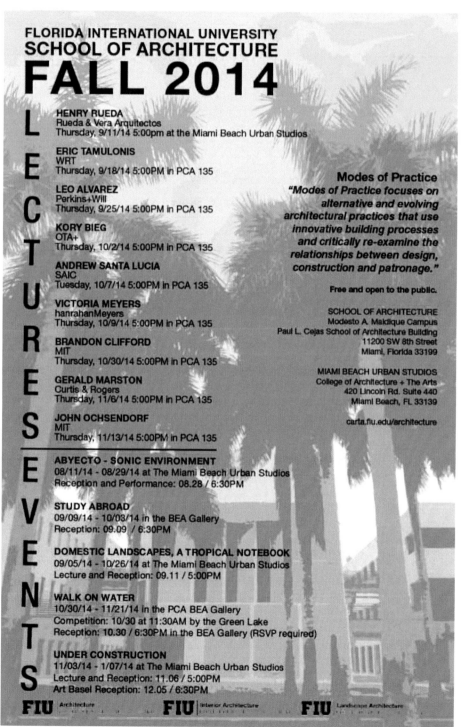

FLORIDA INTERNATIONAL UNIVERSITY
SCHOOL OF ARCHITECTURE
FALL 2014

L E C T U R E S

HENRY RUEDA
Rueda & Vera Arquitectos
Thursday, 9/11/14 5:00pm at the Miami Beach Urban Studios

ERIC TAMULONIS
WRT
Thursday, 9/18/14 5:00PM in PCA 135

LEO ALVAREZ
Perkins+Will
Thursday, 9/25/14 5:00PM in PCA 135

KORY BIEG
OTA+
Thursday, 10/2/14 5:00PM in PCA 135

ANDREW SANTA LUCIA
SAIC
Tuesday, 10/7/14 5:00PM in PCA 135

VICTORIA MEYERS
hanrahanMeyers
Thursday, 10/9/14 5:00PM in PCA 135

BRANDON CLIFFORD
MIT
Thursday, 10/30/14 5:00PM in PCA 135

GERALD MARSTON
Curtis & Rogers
Thursday, 11/6/14 5:00PM in PCA 135

JOHN OCHSENDORF
MIT
Thursday, 11/13/14 5:00PM in PCA 135

E V E N T S

ABYECTO - SONIC ENVIRONMENT
08/11/14 - 08/29/14 at The Miami Beach Urban Studios
Reception and Performance: 08.28 / 6:30PM

STUDY ABROAD
09/09/14 - 10/03/14 in the BEA Gallery
Reception: 09.09 / 6:30PM

DOMESTIC LANDSCAPES, A TROPICAL NOTEBOOK
09/05/14 - 10/26/14 at The Miami Beach Urban Studios
Lecture and Reception: 09.11 / 5:00PM

WALK ON WATER
10/30/14 - 11/21/14 in the PCA BEA Gallery
Competition: 10/30 at 11:30AM by the Green Lake
Reception: 10.30 / 6:30PM in the BEA Gallery (RSVP required)

UNDER CONSTRUCTION
11/03/14 - 1/07/14 at The Miami Beach Urban Studios
Lecture and Reception: 11.06 / 5:00PM
Art Basel Reception: 12.05 / 6:30PM

Modes of Practice
"Modes of Practice focuses on alternative and evolving architectural practices that use innovative building processes and critically re-examine the relationships between design, construction and patronage."

Free and open to the public.

SCHOOL OF ARCHITECTURE
Modesto A. Maidique Campus
Paul L. Cejas School of Architecture Building
11200 SW 8th Street
Miami, Florida 33199

MIAMI BEACH URBAN STUDIOS
College of Architecture + The Arts
420 Lincoln Rd. Suite 440
Miami Beach, FL 33139

carta.fiu.edu/architecture

FIU Architecture　　**FIU** Interior Architecture　　**FIU** Landscape Architecture

Kory Bieg
OTA+

10/02/14 | 5:00pm | PCA 135
With Professor Eric Goldemberg as respondent

Andrew Santa Lucia '10
The School of the Art Institute of Chicago

10/07/14 | 5:00pm | PCA 135
With Professor Jason Chandler as respondent

Brandon Clifford
Matter Design

10/30/14 | 5:00pm | PCA 135
With Professor Nick Gelpi as respondent

Victoria Meyers
hanrahan Meyers architects

10/09/14 | 5:00pm | PCA 135

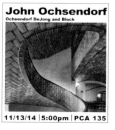

John Ochsendorf
Ochsendorf DeJong and Block

11/13/14 | 5:00pm | PCA 135

Nader Ardalan
Harvard Design School

11/20/14 | 8:00am | PCA 175
With Professor Thomas Spiegelhalter as respondent
ADAPTIVE ARCHITECTURE FOR HOT/ARID & HOT/HUMID REGIONS

FLORIDA
INTERNATIONAL
UNIVERSITY
SCHOOL OF ARCHITECTURE

Spring 2015

January

Events / Exhibitions / **Lecture Series**

15 - March 5
SHALLOW DEPTH: Seeing and Making Miami, Charr's Exhibition
CARTA Miami Beach Urban Studios
Opening Reception:
Thursday, 15
6 pm - 8 pm

20
VisualArq + Grasshopper Workshop
PCA 135
5 pm - 7 pm

22
Constance Silver, M.S.W., PH.D
C.MCSILVER ART
PCA 135
5 pm - 6:15pm
5 pm - 6:15pm
in PCA 135

29
Robert Lloyd
Arquitectonica GEO
5 pm - 6:15 pm
in PCA 135

February

05 - March 06
Leaders of Design, Alumni Exhibition +
Panel Discussion
In conjunction with Panther Alumni Week (PAW)
CARTA Miami Beach Urban Studios
Panel Discussion + Reception:
Thursday, 05
6 pm - 8:30 pm

12
Randy Hollingworth
Bermello Ajamil & Partners, Inc.
5 pm - 6:15 pm
in PCA 135

15 - 20
Cruise Ship and Super Yacht (CSSY)
Cultural Exchange Workshops
PCA 341

19
Liam Obrien
Collective-LOK
5 pm - 6:15 pm
in PCA 135

19 - April 17
SEVEN, A Numbers Game
William O'Brien , Jr. Exhibition
BEA Gallery (PCA 140)
Opening Reception:
Thursday, 19
6:30 pm - 8:30 pm

26
Alastair Gordon
CARTA Dean's Distinguished Fellow
5 pm - 6:15 pm
in PCA 135

03
David Fano, '03- PAW Lecturer
CASE Inc.
5 pm - 6:15 pm
in PCA 135

March

20 - 21
Architecture Americas International
League Summit (ALIAS)
CARTA Miami Beach Urban Studios
Exhibition Opening:
Friday, 20, 6 pm - 7 pm
Workshops: Saturday, 21
9 am - 4 pm

24 - May 15
Lincoln Road Mall Pavilions Morris Lapidus Exhibition Featuring Select Works by FIU Students
CARTA Miami Beach Urban Studios
Opening Reception:
Tuesday, March 24
6 pm - 8 pm

25
Career Fair
Paul L. Cejas School of Architecture Building
10 am - 2 pm

19
Enzo Enea
Enea Landscape Architecture
5 pm - 6:15 pm
in PCA 135

26
Ana Miljacki
MIT
5 pm - 6:15 pm
in PCA 135

April

02
Eco-Couture Recycled Fashion Show
Paul L. Cejas School of Architecture Building
7:30 pm - 11 pm

09 - 10
Interior Architecture Symposium
CARTA Miami Beach Urban Studios

24
Master Project Super Jury
BEA Gallery (PCA 140)
9 am - 5 pm

02
Theo Spyropolous
Minimaforms
5 pm - 6:15 pm
in PCA 135

Location

Florida International University
Modesto A. Maidique Campus
Paul L. Cejas School of Architecture
Building, 11200 S.W. 8th Street
Miami, Florida 333199

Florida International University
College of Architecture + The Arts
Miami Beach Urban Studios
420 Lincoln Road, Suite 440
Miami Beach, Florida 33139
www.carta.fiu.edu

FIU Architecture
FIU Landscape Architecture + Environmental and Urban Design
FIU Interior Architecture

Florida International University
School of Architecture
BUILDING 2050
"SABANA GRANDE BLVD PROJECT"
ELISA SILVA
Principal Architect
VENEZUELA
MARCH 20 - 21, 2015

Florida International University
School of Architecture
BUILDING 2050
"OAXACA SCHOOL OF PLASTIC ARTS"
MAURICIO ROCHA
Architect/ Founder of Taller de Arquitectura- MR
MEXICO
MARCH 20 - 21, 2015

Florida International University
School of Architecture
BUILDING 2050
"UNILEVER"
SOLANO BENITEZ
Architect/ Co-Founder of Gabinete de Arquitectura
PARAGUAY
MARCH 20 - 21, 2015

Florida International University
School of Architecture
BUILDING 2050
"INNOVATION CENTER UC A.A."
JUAN IGNACIO CERDA
Partner Architect of ELEMENTAL
CHILE
MARCH 20 - 21, 2015

Miami 2100

11.07.2014
Coral Gables Museum
Marilys Nepomechie
Eric Peterson

Wall Sound

08.11.2014
MBUS Gallery
Eric Goldemberg

Domestic Landscape

09.11.2014
MBUS Design Gallery
Henry Rueda

Constructing PAMM

11.06.2014
MBUS Design Gallery
Daniel Azoulay

Infill Housing 2

09.05.2014
Coral Gables Museum
FIU SOA

Lincoln Road Follies

03.24.2015
MBUS Design Gallery
Morris Lapidus

7even: A Numbers Game

02.19.2015
MMC BEA Galllery
Lian O'Brian

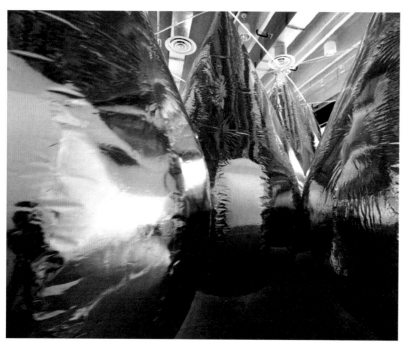

Shallow Depth

03.24.2015
MBUS Main Gallery
Jason Chandler
Roberto Rovira
Jacek Kolasinski

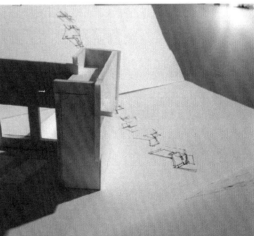

Eco-Couture Fashion Show
April 2nd, 2015

FIU Architecture alumna Amira Ajlouni (M.Arch '14) started Eco-Couture in Spring 2014. At the time, the fashion show was a part of her thesis project, but she has continued it as a new tradition for the FIU School of Architecture, with the help of FIU Architecture student Jennifer Luis. When asked about the genesis of her idea, Ajlouni said that she "wanted people to see recycled materials in a different light....I also wanted people to be inspired....Finally, I wanted to start a tradition." Eco-Couture was created with the purpose of promoting sustainability through fashion. Through collaborative effort from FIU students, the FIU Office of Sustainability, and Florida International University's School of Architecture, Eco-Couture featured the recycled fashion show competition, giveaways of recycled projects, and recycled art installations. Through this event, Eco-Couture strived to educate and inspire the community about good recycling habits and a sustainable lifestyle.

Walk on Water
October 30th, 2014

For the 25th year in a row, FIU Department of Architecture Professor Jaime Canaves challenged his students to create floating shoes and race across a 175-foot-wide campus lake on the north side of the Steve and Dorothea Green Library. The result was Walk on Water, the university tradition that comprised more than 40 students scrambling to cross without getting wet. The first student to cross the lake was Anibal Herrera, who won a $500 scholarship from FIU Architecture. All other students who crossed the lake received an "A" grade for the project and the opportunity to drop their lowest grade. In addition to being a class assignment, Walk on Water was hosted by FIU in commemoration of Architecture and Design Month. This year, FIU President Mark B. Rosenberg and FIU College of Architecture + The Arts Dean Brian Schriner attended the event and supported the participants. The event was covered by the ABC, NBC and CBS Florida news stations and Channel 7 News.

Course
Description

Course Description
Fall 2014

Design 1 | ARC 1301
Nikolay Nedev, Coordinator
Arnaldo Sanchez
Elite Kedan
Emmanuel Ferro
Jorge Balboa
Marco Campa
Sara Garaulet
The first design studio was developed for beginning architecture, landscape architecture, and interior architecture students. The course was designed to immediately engage students in thinking about and making space through drawings and models in a series of exercises. The exercises were set with specific parameters and focused on an analytical, visual design process leading into conceptual development of architectural form and space. Students analyzed visual information and translated 2D interpretations into three dimensional assemblages. The process of assembling became a conceptual operative technique, focusing on connecting conceptual, structural, organizational and spatial terms.

Design 3 | ARC 2303
Eric Peterson, Coordinator
Felice Grodon
Patrick Soares
Site analysis supports and generates a design process for a modest architecturalprogram. Students are introduced to issues involving the analysis of physical site and the cultural framework through which site can be interpreted. Content and issues introduced in the first year are reinforced with the addition of more complex issues and sophisticated questions; architectonic problems become less abstract and students are expected to consider pragmatic issues associated with program, contextual (urban) fabric, and natural systems. A primary goal of the course is to introduce principles and ideas that influence and ultimately shape architecture. The course is divided into sequential design problems that explore architectural space, program, technology and context as critical issues in the design process, as well as potential generators of form. Implicated in the design process are the larger physical and cultural contexts in which architecture is situated.

Formative 1 | ARC 5075
Eric Peterson
The formative studio sequence consisted of three sequential studios that collectively form the foundation of your professional design education. The first half of the semester introduced the basic issues of visualization, spatial definition, spatial organization and parti development. The final project continued these lessons while asking you to engage in a more complex investigation of the issues surrounding the role of site/context, program, typology, precedent, structure and the role of an architectural vocabulary and syntax in the production of architectural form and space. The studio problems strived to introduce and later expand the design vocabulary and strategic repertoire open to each student. This involved projects that addressed problems of architectural design from both the analytic and the synthetic point of view. This will be made manifest through investigating historic precedents with respect to the character of building and spatial organization and through design projects that require the student to speculate and invent.

Design 5 | ARC 5329
Jason Chandler, Coordinator
Adrian Heid
Cynthia Ottchen
Glen Santayana
Jordan Trachtenberg
Nicholas Baker
This semester we examined structure and construction through a series of design projects. The student examined how building buildings work through formal design exercises, a site visit of a significant public building, examination of context, use, history and structure. The semester was divided into four projects. The first three were small-scale spatial interventions for architecturally significant buildings. The fourth project was the design of a public intervention in an architecturally significant building.

Design 7/8 | ARC 5340
Alfredo Andia
Eric Goldemberg
Thomas Spiegelhalter
This studio focused on individual programming, process and design initiatives for diverse artist pavilions for the Lummus Park in South Beach at the Miami Beach Urban Studios. The designs interacted with the landscape and questioned the differences between what is private and public. The unique pavilion and landscape schemes merge together to inhabit the entire existing park. This interaction of ideas created a small artist village where each different art and practice can be projected into the landscape and act as a 365 days community. The Students were required to use intensively the computational capacity for three-dimensional design for the generation of form at the beginning of the design process and carry the 3-D digital exploration and 3-D printing throughout the final representation of the projects. In this studio the students experimented with another way to look at design. They strategized design as catalyst to produce spontaneous life conditions that

will create urbanity via "fascination. The final work focused on generating attention and enthusiasm for the area, redefine its character and the atmosphere in order to attract the cosmopolitan public that flocks to Miami for the mega-events around Art Basel, Ultra, the Boat Show, and the 100 years celebration of Miami Beach in 2015.

Integrated Comprehensive Design | ARC 5361
Henry Rueda, Coordinator
Claudia Busch
Mark Marine
Michael Repovich
Exploration of arch systems; structural, environmental, lifesafety, assembly and enclosure on building form, content and expression. Students will assess and integrate systems into the design process.

Design 10 | ARC 6356
Nick Gelpi
Marilys Nepomechie
This studio established a critical engagement with architecture through a problematizing of the role of experimentation in the studio. Students re-examined the pedagogical approach of the Bauhaus preliminary course titled "Vorkurs." In that Preliminary course, students were asked to suspend disbelief.Three unique instructors each had their own approach to the class, but what they all had in common was the notion that students learned by doing, experimentation for its own sake was encouraged and 'play' was considered key in imparting important theoretical discoveries. This approach is similar to the ambitions of an architectural Mockup, where in order to understand the design fully, it must be executed and built to scale. This suggests there is a level of indeterminacy in the design where representational norms are no longer sufficient. This course will ask students to produce their own indeterminacies in the process of play, progressing from something preconceived to the intentional shedding of preconceptions in the pursuit of new insights into new capacities and potentials. With the Vorkurs in mind we can situate the notion of large scale mockups as examples of experimentation in which thinking is building, and building is play for the sake of experimentation. Shouldn't contemporary design build incorporate more aspects of play, destabilizing the conventional methods of construction and assembly? When Josef Albers taught the 3rd installment of the Vorkurs class, students would visit workshops such as cabinet makers, wall paper factories, even breweries to criticize and rethink their manufacturing procedures. The expected outcomes of this type of measured play are for a new type of practice where the architect looks for evidence outside the normal conventions of practice abandoning preconceptions,

producing new entanglements with reality both expected and even hopefully anticipated. This course suggests that learning in the studio happens not in the final solution to the given program, rather in the insight produced by the process of building, mocking, and playing.

Design 10 | ARC 6356
Marilys Nepomechie

Our work contributed to a series of visioning exercise for the Miami/ Miami Beach of the next 100 years: International, culturally complex, multi-centered, growing in density –and lacking adequate infrastructure for optimal connectivity and operation.

Fundamentals of Digital Design | ARC 4058
Nick Gelpi
The course was organized as a series of software introductions and exercises intended to both introduce the basics of digital representation, as well as present a platform for investigating architecture through the use of digital tools. Students were guided through a sequence of exercises, each building in complexity, culminating in a final project which will combine the in dividual topics and skills explored throughout the semester. Students began the course by learning the standards and conventions of 2PDimensional drawing in Autocad, and then progress to 3Dimensional Modelling in Rhinoceros. Students then learned the basics of materializing there drawings through a series introductions to digital fabrication tools including Lasercutting, 3D Printing, and CNC Milling. The course was intended to familiarize students with these conventions,as well as provide graphic presentation principles such as Drawing Layout, rendering, lighting conditions, camera setup, the basics of material emulation, and digital fabrication.

Enviromental Systems in Architecture 1 | ARC 5612
Thomas Spiegelhalter
The course was intended to familiarize the student with saving resources using passive and active integrated building technology systems (thermal, electrical, mechanical systems) within the architectural design process.

Introduction to Architectural Theories | ARC 5249
Gray Read
In this large, required course we asked, "what does a building do in the world?" Through a series of readings, discussions, and exercises, we considered how buildings interact with people socially and how they modify their surroundings environmentally. Each student pursued these two questions through study of

a single building of his or her choice, developing analytical drawings, then writing papers that explain their findings. The class read key texts that construct the context for their investigations. In the first half of the class we consider the role buildings take in the social world. In readings and discussions we considered how they place, group and present people in the events that make up our lives. In a series of in-class exercises students developed analytical drawings that show the social strategies of design. In the second half of the class, we looked at the environmental impact of buildings. We read and discussed texts that explain the current environmental crisis as well as design strategies to address it. In-class exercises developed techniques of representation that make a building's performance visible. In using these tools of analysis on their chosen buildings, students develop an investigative approach to design.

Integrated Building Systems | ARC 5483
Claudia Busch
Mark Marine
This course aimed to provide an understanding of how the selection and integration of building systems in the early stages of the design process will lead to production of resource efficient buildings with minimal adverse impact on the environment. The course approached the integration of building technology and architectural design by defining them as mutually supportive thought processes. The course designed to guide students to consciously develop an approach to the disposition of structure, environmental systems, materials, connections, details, etc. supportive and expressive of the design proposals they have developed in their concurrent design studios. The course assignments will be closely linked to the studio design and production activities.

Pedagogy Seminar | ARC 5943
Gray Read
This elective seminar course served the many advanced students, particularly MAA students, who assist in teaching courses, either as studio instructors, discussion section leaders, or faculty assistants. It offered a focused study of teaching philosophy and techniques, with special consideration of studio instruction, as well as a forum for discussing their experiences as first-time teachers. Each class meeting is planned and run by a student or team of students who present the weekly topic and offer prepared discussion questions or exercises for the group. Guest discussants joined the group several times during the semester to bring their experience to the table. In addition, each student researched a topic drawn from the course to which he or she

is assigned and presents it to the class as if giving a class lecture. The group then gives constructive feedback to help the presenter understand what students might actually learn from the presentation and suggestions on how to improve the lecture. Finally students submitted a term paper on their research topic. In this class all students were teachers and the shifting roles helps the group reflect on the process of learning as well as teaching.

Course Description Spring 2015

Research Methods | ARC 6947

David Rifkind
Gray Read
Winifred Newman

The only required course for incoming MAA students, this seminar reviewed techniques for architectural research and methods for analyzing information. Three professors in History/Theory/Criticism each taught a module of the course in sequence, giving students three distinct approaches to scholarly work. The first module taught by Dr. Read centers on how to structure questions for research that are both meaningful as building blocks toward answering large questions in the field and answerable within the resources and constraints of the MAA program. The second module taught by Dr. Rifkind reviews several approaches that scholars take to analyze historical phenomena, each focusing on specific types of information out of the broad array of available data in order to gain insight into a large question. The third module taught by Dr. Newman focuses on techniques of analysis, sources and methods of organizing quantitative and qualitative data for a proposal. Throughout the course students revise and refine their own MAA project proposal, focusing the topic, gathering resources, and developing working methods that they will use to pursue independent work.

Design 2 | ARC 1302

Nikolay Nedev, Coordinator
Elite Kedan
Emmanuel Ferro
Felice Grodin
Jorge Balboa
Marco Campa
Sara Garaulet

Design Studio 2 continued to explore the definition, understanding, and creation of space by utilizing a series of concise exercises. In the first assignment, students were introduced to principles of proportion and scale with an emphasis on the relationship between the body and three-dimensional space. Research, analysis, and drawing were approached with the intention of using the understanding of those geometric and proportional systems as formal and conceptual space-making tools. Students further analyze poetic implications of movement, thresholds + transitions, spatial framing + extension, as well as tectonic notions of connections, joints, and preliminary ideas of structure and materiality. Throughout the semester, the assignments increased in complexity as we introduced different program and scales.

These abstract design exercises combine research with a rigorous method of developing layered drawings and models.

Design 4 | ARC 2304

Nick Gelpi, Coordinator
Andrea Perelli
Jeff Lodin

The main objective of design 4 was to introduce principles and ideas that influenced and ultimately shaped architecture in terms of the implications of the larger physical and cultural context. The course was divided into sequential problems that explore architectural space as a result of contextual forces. The city was introduced as a starting point for the exploration of these spatial, social, political and cultural contextual forces. Projects engaged the structure and the fabric of the city with its attendant issues of public/private, fabric/space, interior/exterior. Site, social and cultural issues were the generator for design projects with repetitive spatial and programmatic elements. Studio emphasized design process and relationship between conceptual design, structural systems, materials and details.

Design 6 | ARC 5335

Jason Chandler, Coordinator
Adam Drisin
Armando Rigau
Cynthia Ottchen
Glenda Puente
Nathaly Haratz

This semester sought to examine housing. The student designed a comprehensive housing project in an urban context. The semester was divided into three projects. The first project was the documentation of Miami infill buildings. The second project was the documentation and analysis of housing typologies in Savannah, Georgia. Infill party wall housing was explored in third project through a major design project sited in Miami, Florida. Throughout the semester, the studio was concerned with the organizations and studied adjacencies of living. The concept of living and providing of its meaningful shelter will be explored as a seamless event that included many scales: from the scale of the city down to the scale of furniture.

Design 9 | ARC 5362
Gray Read, Coordinator
Thomas Spiegelhalter, Coordinator
Henry Rueda
Claudia Busch
Architectural Design 9 focused on developing strategies for sustainable design which engaged the landscape and the city. The studio was coordinated with the Department of Landscape Architecture and included four lectures on landscape topics and an in-class workshop. The project explored ideas of small size/ big impact urban artifacts that will demonstrate the challenges of designing urban conditions in a net-zero sustainable Downtown Miami and Miami River area.

Masters Project | ARC 6970
Alfredo Andia
Camilo Rosales
Eric Peterson
Eric Goldemberg
Jaime Canaves
Malik Benjamin
Marilys Nepomechie
The final studio in the Graduate Design sequence encouraged students to engage in increasingly independent work that will be presented in both a review and a final book outlining their process over the course of the semester and their final designs. The Masters Project addressed questions, as appropriate, related to the changing character of the city, the nature of social/cultural institutions, and the context in which their project is situated. The area of research was developed into highly articulated projects. These expressed a substantial degree of resolution and was presented with attention to all aspects of design from technical details to overall planning. The projects advanced all areas covered in the comprehensive studio (including building systems, ADA, and safety). The student work also considered issues of sustainability, ethics, cost analysis, and materiality.

Furniture Design | ARC 5935
Eric Peterson
This course was a workshop based design/build class for the fabrication of three significant working furniture prototypes. This semester we fabricated furniture for Whole Foods Market South Beach. The fabrication method was based on adaptive reuse of discarded shipping pallets and other discarded materials. The design intention was to develop and test fabrication systems to work with low grade materials and apply them to three different furniture pieces. We fabricated a community table, an exterior bench, and a couch and table for the employee break room.

Graphics 2 | ARC 1132
Nikolay Nedev, Coordinator
Elite Kedan
Emmanuel Ferro
Felice Grodin
Jorge Balboa
Marco Campa
Sara Garaulet
The second design Graphic Course highlights the understanding how to express graphically relevant ideas using different medias. The course starts to explore the use of perspectives as a representation tool for different stages of the design process. Students engage in different methodologies using digital techniques and graphic software, such as illustrator, photoshop and InDesign. The intention is to emphasize on a menu of techniques that will prepare the student to use digital software as a communication tool throughout their architectural education. As a final project students have to produce a catalog of their work.

Professional Office Practice | ARC 6280
Alfredo Andia
Study of the ethical, legal, financial, and managerial aspects of professional practice in architecture.

Mapping: Applied Theory | ARC 5935
Winifred E Newman
Mapping reveals the complex relationship between representation and thinking, technology, culture and aesthetic practices. Embedded in the discussion were the general terms of cartography and how mapping re-constructs a three-dimensional world onto a surface. We addressed the map both as a text and as an object of historical explanation from which we can gain a better understanding of current spatial practices. With the aim of developing more effective ways to employ mapping, this course looked at maps in relation to the cartographic histories associated with the form of the map used (ichnographic, cognitive, photogrammetric) and the relationship of these maps to place. We focused on mapping as a strategy for calibrating conditions of understanding place.

Methods and Materials of Construction 2 | ARC 5467

Nikolay Nedev

The class examined building construction by individual material types: wood, brick, stone, steel, concrete, pre-cast concrete, and glass. A study of the types of construction and materials used in institutional, residential, multi-residential and office buildings assemblies of moderate and heavy construction. How materials are properly installed and inspected, including the use of special equipment, in accordance to drawings, specifications, codes, standards, and agency recommendations. Integration of building technologies and assemblies to Architectural Design.

Toys, Tables, Walkers and Widgets: Industrial Design Applications in Occupational Therapy | ARC 5935

Winifred E Newman

This course focused on the problems of spatial syntax for a particular user group. Students in architecture worked together to understand the functional needs of people with a variety of neurological and physical challenges, propose to improve upon or design new devices based on a rigorous analysis of patient needs, therapeutic outcomes and potential patent development. Students learned to document and analyze findings, prepare and make material samples of propositions, and present work and findings to a professional organization. Topics covered included spatial syntax, isovist analysis, ergonomics, functionality, aesthetics, and usability (user-interface) of objects.

Enviromental Systems in Architecture 2 | ARC 5612

Thomas Spiegelhalter

The course was mainly focused on advanced parametric, climate-responsive, carbon-neutral and resource efficient environmental concepts, optimization, zoning, control and building design strategy modeling for operiational building service and comfort. The lectures, workshops, field trips and exercises were supported with multiple 2-D/3-D software tools and cloud-service platforms. All concepts and learning objectives for parametric-algorithmic passive and active in-put analysis, zoning, calculation and design strategy modelling were centered around the following major areas: Sustainable, carbon-neutral design context and load analysis modeling; passive and active hybrid thermal design, space conditioning sizing and control; natural and artificial illumination analysis and design; acoustic concepts and design; water harnessing, black/gray/rain-water treating, recycling, re-use and distribution systems; fire protection and systems design; electricity service and distribution systems; renewable energy generation, micro and large-scale infrastructure sizing and distribution systems (buildings and cities as power plants); total building automation systems and building information systems(sensor/signal systems for different intelligent building typologies) ; X-Y-Z spatial transportation systems (load analysis and spatial requirements), and final studiointegrated research projects for whole building analysis, carbon-neutral systems design and performance evaluation.

Student Organizations 2014-2015

Student Leadership

American Institute of Architecture Students
President: Carla Escobar
Vice President: Brad Alvarez
Social Chair: Victoria Gomes
CSO Representative: Zair Toloza
Secretary: Gabriela Soto
Faculty Advisor: Jaime Canaves
http://aias.org/

Alpha Rho Chi
Worthy Architect (President): Michael Peisel
Worthy Associate Architect (Vice President):
Agustin Martins
Worthy Scribe (Secretary): Brian Rivera
Worthy Clerk (Secretary): Anica Lompre
Worthy Estimator (Treasurer): Luis Marenco
Superintendent: Maria Sol Rivera
Sergeant-in-Arms: Ruben Pacheco
Faculty Advisor: Malik Benjamin
http://www.apxnicon.com

The National Organization of Minority
Architect Students
President: Santasha Hart
Vice President: Alexa Marie-Monfort
CSO Representative: Jorge Rodriguez
Secretary: Jasmin Jenkins
Faculty Advisor: Mark Marine
http://nomas.fiu.edu/about-us/

Tau Sigma Delta Honor Society
President: Andrea Rivera
Vice President: Monica Vega
Secretary: Ruth Brooks
Treasurer: Carla Escobar
Faculty Advisor: Professor Marilys
Nepomechie
http://www.tausigmadelta.org/opmanual.htm

American Institute of Architecture Students (AIAS)

The American Institute of Architecture Students is an independent, nonprofit, student-run organization dedicated to providing unmatched programs, information, and resources on issues critical to architectural education. The mission of the AIAS is to promote excellence in architectural education, training, and practice; to foster an appreciation of architecture and related disciplines; to enrich communities in a spirit of collaboration; and to organize students and combine their efforts to advance the art and science of architecture. The mission of the AIAS is:

To promote excellence in architecture education, training and practice. Members of the AIAS have the opportunity to have their work publicized.

To foster an appreciation of architecture and related disciplines. We host events that provides students with the opportunity to learn about the issues facing architectural education and the profession, to meet students and professionals with common interests, and to interact with some of today's leading architects and designers.

To enrich communities in a spirit of collaboration. We are organizing our members to be good citizens in their communities.

To organize students and combine their efforts to advance the art and science of architecture. We serve as the sole student voice in the decision making process of such organizations as AIA, ACSA, and NAAB.

Alpha Rho Chi

The Alpha Rho Chi Foundation was established in 1989 to advance education and research directed toward the discovery, promotion, furtherance and dissemination of knowledge related to architecture and the allied arts. To that end, the APX Foundation provides scholarships for Alpha Rho Chi members; sponsors professional programs at many levels; underwrites scholarly publications and the Alpha Rho Chi Medal program which recognizes leadership, scholarship, and service in students in both the US and Canada; and promotes new and innovative educational opportunities for students in architecture and the allied arts.

National Organization of Minority Architect Students (NOMA)

Aims and Objectives

The National Organization of Minority Architects has been organized to:
· Foster communications and fellowship among minority architects;
· Form a federation of existing and proposed local minority architectural groups;
· Fight Discrimination and other selection policies being used by public and private sector clients to unfairly restrict minority architects' participation in design and construction;
· Act as a clearing house for information and maintain a roster on practitioners;
· Promote the design and development of living, working, and recreational environments of the highest quality;
· Create and maintain relationships with other professionals and technicians whose work affects the physical and social environment;
· Encourage the establishment of coalitions of member firms and individuals to form associate and joint venture relationships;
· Speak with a common voice on public policy;

· Work with local, state, and national governments on issues affecting the physical development of neighborhoods and communities;
· Be an effective source of motivation and inspiration for minority youth.

Tau Sigma Delta Honor Society

Tau Sigma Delta was organized in 1913 at the University of Michigan at the suggestion and guidance of the faculty in Architecture and Landscape Design who selected the first group of senior honor students to be the founding members. After three years of trial, the system of elections was extended to other universities.

With gradual growth, it became necessary for the best interests of the schools at which chapters became located, to extend elections to honor students who were majoring in a degree in departments allied with Architecture and Landscape Architecture. Thus Tau Sigma Delta developed from a senior honor society in Architecture and Landscape Architecture to become inclusive of upper level undergraduate and graduate

students in Architecture, Architectural Engineering, Architectural Design, Landscape Architecture, Visual Arts, Planning, Decorative Design, Interior Design, Industrial Design and all the arts allied with Architecture

Tau Sigma Delta proved its worth steadily. It overcame the obstacles precipitated by World War I, the subsequent inflationary period, and the resultant era of world economic "recession and adjustment," a nd the later effects of World War II. To be sure, progress was delayed by these crucial tests of the times, and four of its chapters became inactive; however, the Society emerged strengthened by those tests.

Another test for the society came during the Vietnam Conflict. Membership in the society declined with several chapters becoming inactive. This has reversed itself in the past few years with the number of new chapters reaching an all time high.

NAAB
Statement And Degree

In the United States, most registration boards require a degree from an accredited professional degree program as a prerequisite for licensure. The National Architectural Accrediting Board (NAAB), which is the sole agency authorized to accredit professional degree programs in architecture offered by institutions with U.S. regional accreditation, recognizes three types of degrees: the Bachelor of Architecture, the Master of Architecture, and the Doctor of Architecture. A program may be granted an eight-year, three-year, or two-year term of accreditation, depending on the extent of its conformance with established educational standards.

Doctor of Architecture and Master of Architecture degree programs may require a preprofessional undergraduate degree in architecture for admission. However, the preprofessional degree is not, by itself, recognized as an accredited degree.

Florida International University, College of Architecture + The Arts, Department of Architecture offers the following NAAB-accredited degree programs:

M. Arch.
(high school degree + 175 credits)

M. Arch.
(pre-professional degree + 60 credits)

M. Arch.
(non-pre-professional degree + 105 credits)

Next accreditation visit: 2017.

Applying to the Architecture program involves two steps: first, apply to the University, and second, submit your portfolio to the Architecture Department for review by the departmental admissions committee. The Architecture Department admits students into the Master of Architecture program at different levels, depending on degree background.

Architecture Department Admissions Officer
Adrian Molina, amolina@fiu.edu

Admissions

Freshmen Applicants

For students seeking to begin their professional design studies as undergraduates, the Architecture Department offers the Undergraduate M.Arch 5.

Applicants who have recently graduated from high school begin with admission at the freshman year. These pre-graduate students are admitted into the foundational curriculum of the undergraduate M.Arch degree program. Pre-graduate students progress through the foundational design course work and general education studies (73 credit hours) and those students who successfully complete the pre-graduate foundation seamlessly matriculate into graduate coursework and receive the Master of Architecture degree at the conclusion of an 102 additional credit hours.

No baccalaureate degree is awarded on this path. The course of study takes five or six years to complete, depending on the track that is selected.

· Total Undergraduate credits   73
· Total Graduate Degree Credits   102
· Total Credits to AccMLA   175

A transition from undergraduate to graduate standing occurs at the end of the fourth year Spring semester after the completion of 120 credits. Students must be in good standing with a minimum cumulative GPA of 3.0 or better. A Bachelor degree is not awarded at any point in the program.

Transfer Applicants

Applicants who possess an AA degree in Architecture, may also apply for the Master of Architecture degree program. These students apply to the Undergraduate M.Arch 5 path and, if accepted, will transfer in at the third year and take 102 credit hours of graduate level course work. Then, they will receive the Master of Architecture degree. The course of study usually takes three to four years to complete, depending on the track that is selected.
Transfer students who have not completed the Pre-Graduate Foundation courses may not begin the studio sequence until completed.

M.Arch 3-Year Applicants

The three-year Master of Architecture program (M.Arch) is for applicants with no background in architecture, and who possess a four-year undergraduate degree in any area other than architecture. The three-year Master of Architecture program is also for applicants with foreign degrees, including foreign degrees in architecture.

The program consists of 105 credit hours and is usually completed in three and one-half years. The course of study consists of six semesters of design studio course work followed by a semester-long Master's project. Supporting courses in history and theory, building technology, sustainability practices, digital technology, professional business practices as well as cross-disciplinary electives complete the course of study. Students are eligible to spend their sixth semester studying in Genoa, Italy.

M.Arch 2-Year Applicants

The two-year Master of Architecture program (M.Arch) is for applicants who have earned the pre-professional four-year undergraduate degree in architecture as part of the 4+2 combined degree path. Students in this path continue their architectural education by following a course of 60 graduate credit hours in a professional program. Students are given the appropriate level of advanced standing for professional course content already taken as part of their pre-professional four-year degree. The course of study consists of three semesters of design studio course work followed by a semester long master's project.

Supporting courses in history and theory, building technology, sustainability practices, digital technology, professional business practices as well as cross-disciplinary electives complete the degree program. Students are eligible to spend a semester studying in Genoa, Italy.

Master of Arts in Architecture – MAA - 1 Year Applicants

The Master of Arts in Architecture is a 36-credit post- professional degree program that enables students to pursue advanced studies in three areas: theory, applied research and special topics in practice. Individual areas of concentration are pursued through course work and independent study and may include the philosophy and history of design, digital technologies and visualization, mapping, technology, sustainability, neuroscience and architecture, furniture and industrial design, advanced topics in design and sustainable development. These concentration areas are supported by focus topics in the FIU SOA curriculum and allow students to pursue advanced research combining cross-disciplinary course work with faculty areas of specialization.

Research Options

Students seeking to conduct non studio-based research have the option to complete either a thesis or a research project.Students opting to complete a thesis must submit a thesis proposal prior to their final semester. Students seeking to conduct studio-based research must complete a master's project.

Areas of Specialization

Students may choose a course of study that is either studio-based or non-studio-based. Any of the following areas of specialization may be chosen for either a studio- based or non-studio-based course of study.

· Theoretical Research
Aesthetics and Politics, History and Philosophy
of Design

· Applied Research
Digital Technologies and Visualization, Mapping with a GIS
Certificate Option, Technology and Sustainability, Furniture and
Industrial Design, Neuroscience and Architecture, Advanced
Design Studies

· Advanced Topics in Design

Graduate Certificate In The History, Theory And Criticism Of Architecture

The Graduate Certificate in the History, Theory and Criticism of Architecture offers exceptional students enrolled in degree programs in the School of Architecture and the university community a chance to follow a rigorous course of study in history, theory and criticism, including a required seminar devoted to research methodologies. For architecture students, we offer the further option of a pedagogical apprenticeship, where faculty members mentor students seeking to become teachers. For students outside the School of Architecture, we offer an opportunity to supplement their studies in history, anthropology, environmental science, art history, literature, area studies and other fields with an intense and systematic engagement with cultural production and the visual arts. The certificate program helps students hone their critical skills as they generate new knowledge and embark on self-directed research. Students admitted to a graduate degree program at FIU may apply for admission to the Graduate Certificate in the History, Theory and Criticism of Architecture.

Department of Architecture

School of Architecture

Jason Chandler
Chair and Associate Professor
305 348 6913
chandler@fiu.edu

Maria D. Garcia
Office Assistant for the
Department of Architecture
305 348 1323
garciamd@fiu.edu

Madeleine Manzano-Barrera
Office Assistant
305 348 8130
mmanzano@fiu.edu

Advising
Aisha L. Williams
Academic Advisor
Student Services and Advising
Center College of Architecture + The Arts
305 348 3007
aiwillia@fiu.edu

Digital Laboratory
Mike Bisnett
Digital Laboratory Assistant
305 348 2960
mbisnett@fiu.edu

Media and Marketing
Juan Brizuela
Media & Marketing Coordinator College
of Architecture + The Arts
jbrizuel@fiu.edu

Miami Beach Urban Studios

John Stuart
Associate Dean For Cultural
And Community Engagement
Exectutive Director
305 535 1460
stuartj@fiu.edu

Jacqueline Thompson
Office Manager
305 535 1463
janthomp@fiu.edu

Acknowledgements

Image Credits
Robin Hill
Manuel Perez-Trujillo
Michael Flores
Juan Brizuela
Marny Pereda

Design by
Fonte: Raúl Lira

Guests
Barbara De Vries
Alastair Gordon
Mitchell Kaplan
Amalia Caputo
Raul Lira
Amanda Keeley

Adam Bierman
Jennifer Doval
Juan Fernandez
Daniela Galvan
Nicholas Pendas
Marny Pereda
Adan Quesada
Cesar Ramos-Moron
Amaru Rios
Bobbie Walker
Guillermo Wong
Pierina Yen
Jennifer Kramer
Luisa Arroyo
Luca Di Giacomo
Jose Estrada
Amanda Rhaka Guyah
Yaima Juan
Michael Lassandro
Pedro Lenartowicz
Jennifer Luis
Nicole Mcdaniel
Sean Paul Muiznieks
Byron Munoz

Glenn Munoz
Mario Ortiz
Catherine Pageau
Amaru Rios
Felicito Rodriguez
Esther Roger
Adriana Marie Rojas
Fiorella Salamanca
David Santana
Hassan Sarfraz
Maria Paula Soler
Sandy Suarez
Arny Tejeda
Apoorva Varun Kulkarni
Teri Watson

FIU Architecture
FLORIDA INTERNATIONAL UNIVERSITY